COUNSELING IN CORRECTIONAL ENVIRONMENTS

New Vistas in Counseling Series
Series Editors—Garry Walz and Libby Benjamin
In collaboration with ERIC Counseling and Personnel Services Information Center

Structured Groups for Facilitating Development: Acquiring Life Skills, Resolving Life Themes, and Making Life Transitions, Volume 1
Drum, D. J., Ph.D. and Knott, J. E., Ph.D.

New Methods for Delivering Human Services, Volume 2
Jones, G. B., Ph.D., Dayton, C., Ph.D. and Gelatt, H. B., Ph.D.

Systems Change Strategies in Educational Settings, Volume 3
Arends, R. I., Ph.D. and Arends, J. H., Ph.D.

Counseling Older Persons: Careers, Retirement, Dying, Volume 4
Sinick, D., Ph.D.

Parent Education and Elementary Counseling, Volume 5
Lamb, J. and Lamb, W., Ph.D.

Counseling in Correctional Environments, Volume 6
Bennett, L. A., Ph.D., Rosenbaum, T. S., Ph.D. and McCullough, W. R., Ph.D.

Transcultural Counseling: Needs, Programs and Techniques, Volume 7
Walz, G., Ph.D., Benjamin, L., Ph.D., et al.

Career Resource Centers, Volume 8
Meerbach, J., Ph.D.

Behavior Modification Handbook for Helping Professionals, Volume 9
Mehrabian, A., Ph.D.

Counseling in Correctional Environments

Lawrence A. Bennett, Ph.D.
California Department of Corrections, Sacramento
Thomas S. Rosenbaum, Ph.D.
Milan Federal Correctional Institution, Milan, Michigan
Wayne R. McCullough, Ph.D.
University of Michigan, Ann Arbor

*Vol. 6 in the New Vistas in Counseling Series,
in collaboration with ERIC Counseling and Personnel
Services Information Center
Series Editors*—Garry Walz and Libby Benjamin

HUMAN SCIENCES PRESS
72 Fifth Avenue   3 Henrietta Street
NEW YORK, NY 10011 ● LONDON, WC2E 8LU

Library of Congress Catalog Number 7721269
ISBN: 0-87705-319-7

Copyright © 1978 Human Sciences Press
72 Fifth Avenue, New York, N.Y. 10011

Copyright is claimed until 1983. Thereafter, all portions of the work covered by this copyright will be in the public domain. This work was developed under a contract with the National Institute of Education, Department of Health, Education, and Welfare. However, the content does not necessarily reflect the position or policy of that agency, and no United States Government endorsement of these materials should be inferred.

Printed in the United States of America
89 987654321

Library of Congress Cataloging in Publication Data

Bennett, Lawrence A
  Counseling in correctional environments.

(New vistas in counseling series ; v. 6)
  Includes bibliographical references.
  1. Correctional psychology. 2. Counseling.
I. Rosenbaum, Thomas S., joint author. II. McCullough, Wayne R., joint author. III. Title. IV. Series: New vistas in counseling ; v. 6.
HV9275.B45   365'.66   77-21269
ISBN 0-87705-319-7

TABLE OF CONTENTS

Foreword	7
1. Historical Overview of Correctional Counseling	9
Brief Historical Review	11
Settings for Counseling	13
Summary	19
2. Approaches To Counseling in the Correctional Setting	20
Individual Counseling	20
Group Counseling	21
Client-Centered Counseling	28
Family Counseling	37
Large Group Interaction (Community Living Groups)	39
Summary	44

3. **Differing Objectives** 46
   Career Guidance 47
   Emotional Reorientation 51
   Summary 55
4. **Different Settings** 56
   Probation 56
   Parole 60
   Summary 61
5. **The Differing Levels** 62
   Local Efforts 62
   State Programs 63
   The Federal System 63
   Summary 64
6. **New Approaches** 65
   Group Homes 65
   Matching Client and Counselor 66
   Use of Testing in Counseling 68
   Peer Counseling 70
   Summary 72
7. **Studies of Effectiveness** 73
   The Highfields Program 75
   Lamar Empey 77
   The Youth Center Research Project 77
   Summary 79
8. **Some Practical Guides Toward Application** 81
   Examine the Clientele 81
   Outline Your Objectives 82
   Survey Counseling Approaches 83
   An Overview 88
References 90

FOREWORD

You see, our sensing network revealed that counselors wanted to know about new developments in counseling offenders, both at the state and national levels. So we searched the ERIC system for people and programs and identified Dr. Bennett, then of the California Department of Corrections (now Director of the Center for the Study of Crime, Delinquency and Corrections at Southern Illinois University), as one who was highly knowledgeable about what was happening in state prisons. In the review process, Dr. Rosenbaum of the Milan (Michigan) Federal Correctional Institution made such cogent comments about federal programs that we commissioned him and his colleague, Dr. Wayne McCullough, to provide content from the national perspective. And then it was our task to combine the two manuscripts into one cohesive document. That they meshed so well was gratifying, and we think the outcome is a substantive description of what is really happening in correctional counseling.

Current correctional counseling theory embraces the

concept that offenders are neither mentally ill nor emotionally disturbed, neither "sick" nor incurably "bad." Rather, offenders are viewed as persons who have not had the advantage of positive social models, are extremely limited in their repertoire of appropriate behaviors, and may, in fact, be responding to situational and internal presses in the only ways they know. This more enlightened approach to rehabilitating offenders calls for the development of more humanistic environments. a variety of treatment interventions geared to individual client needs, and integrated programs designed to facilitate the learning of appropriate social skills.

This monograph examines current counseling methods and describes new and emerging approaches such as peer counseling programs, group homes, matching client and counselor, and therapeutic communities. Attention is given to the role of the counselor in such efforts, which can range from personal family friend to designer and evaluator of a complex program; and to the counselor's work setting, which may be in a parolee's home, in a half-way house, or within prison walls. Research studies of the efficacy of correctional counseling are also cited. Although the positive effects of correctional counseling have yet to be demonstrated in experimental studies, there are indications that specific, targeted treatment strategies do make a difference, and sometimes a significant one.

The authors have treated a difficult subject objectively and factually. They have not tried to make exaggerated claims for counseling gains or to suggest that there is one miracle method for dealing with offenders. Out of the thoughtful analysis presented here may very well come the new insights necessary to help custodial counseling fulfill its potential.

Garry R. Walz
Libby Benjamin

Chapter 1

HISTORICAL OVERVIEW OF CORRECTIONAL COUNSELING

This chapter reviews a brief history of counseling in the correctional setting, tracing its development from the early 1900's to the present. It includes brief descriptions of the various settings in which counseling occurs, the vast differences in the clientele, and the widely different approaches used in counseling efforts. Some erroneous assumptions that have persisted through the years are also examined. Plausible reasons for criminal behaviors are briefly explained.

For the last 200 years, workers in the field of crime and punishment have struggled more systematically to find ways of motivating offenders to modify their behavior toward greater social conformity. When the training model emerged in the early 1900's, it represented a departure from the earlier belief that punishment, in and of itself, was sufficient to insure that people would change the manner of their attempts to solve their social problems. Following the disillusionment with the failure of vocational training to cure social ills, "treatment" entered the field. This approach was introduced by religionists and given major impetus by the psychiatric profession, but now it, too, has come to be doubted. Several investigators have questioned whether *any* training or treatment approach can affect the subsequent adjustment of criminals. Despite these attacks, which are becoming more numerous and are being voiced by individuals in high places, correctional workers, probation officers, parole agents, correctional counselors, and correctional officers continue to maintain the belief that something *can* be done. This monograph will outline some of those efforts toward that end, particularly those related to activities that can be classified as counseling.

Traditionally, the initial approach to a problem must be in terms of definition. We are already in trouble, for while "counseling" may be easily *described,* it is not as easily *defined.* On the one hand, the activities that might be characterized as counseling blend into more detailed, intensive activities that are called psychotherapy. On the other hand, the applications of some psychotherapeutic methods such as behavior modification may be included within an individual counseling framework.

For the purposes of this discussion, the following is a working definition of counseling: Planned interaction between the correctional worker and a client or group of clients—probationers, prisoners, or parolees—with the aim of changing the pattern of the recipients' behavior toward conformity to social expectation.

It should be noted that this does not clearly separate counseling activities from psychotherapy. But we may make the assumption that psychotherapy is aimed at resolving internal, personal problems which may be related to delinquent and criminal behavior, and that it is carried out by a professional psychiatrist, psychologist, or social worker specifically trained for this activity. This assumption will be explained in more detail later as basic assumptions are examined.

In addition to providing a current overview of what is going on in correctional counseling, this monograph will present general guidelines to the different approaches that might be initiated in correctional settings. Also, the various settings within which counseling is now taking place will be examined. Since the correctional apparatus has been stratified along the lines of governmental structure, variations related to these different levels will be explored.

Clients of the correctional system are individuals with unique needs. While some counseling approaches involve individualized treatment programs, more and more institutions are becoming unable to provide that level of counseling. Rather, clients with different characteristics are being grouped together. Various counseling practices associated with these subgroups of counselees will be described.

Diversity of treatment approaches has already been suggested by the discussion. The variations and similarities among the numerous approaches will be discussed and innovative approaches identified. Evaluation of correctional programs is ascending; and counseling efforts, like any other program, should be evaluated in terms of benefit, value, and impact. Selective research in the area of counseling will be reviewed as well as suggestions for improving the evaluative process.

Brief Historical Review

Counseling, as such, did not emerge as an unique and separate program until the early 1900's. However, it seems likely that since the earliest days of the penitentiary system in the United States, some form of counseling between religious leaders and inmates took place.

Present day group counseling and its variations are an outgrowth of psychotherapeutic efforts developed by psychologists and psychiatrists. Slavson and Moreno both claim credit for the development of group techniques—Moreno (1957) in the area of psychodrama and Slavson (1950) in role-playing behavior with children. Group therapy became more widely used following World War II when practical needs dictated that some method be developed to use the available professional talents more efficiently. While Slavson and Moreno viewed group work as a therapy of choice, subsequent applications were unfortunately based on sheer economics. That is, group treatment approaches were substituted for individual ones on the basis that in a given hour of a professional's time, eight to ten more clients could be seen.

Group counseling entered the prison systems of the nation sometime in the early 1940's. It was introduced in California, in 1944, into the Reception Center at San Quentin. Certified teachers with some training in educational counseling conducted the groups. Sometimes called "social living," the procedures included lectures as well as discussions and emotional interchanges (Fenton, 1961).

By the early 1950's counseling activities were beginning to expand. One of the most ambitious programs was initiated by Dr. Norman Fenton in California in 1954. It centered on a strong training program, followed by apprenticeship/supervision. Conducting groups were a wide variety of workers—vocational instructors, correctional officers, tradesmen, work foremen, and clerical workers, as well as academic teachers. Once it was developed, the counseling program involved well over 50% of the inmate population. By 1961 an impressive 10,000 inmates and 700 employees were participating each week in group counseling in the California prison system (Fenton, 1961). However, only about 8% of correctional and penal institutions reported that group therapy was a portion of their program, according to a survey made by the American Group Psychotherapy Association in 1950 (Sandhu, 1974).

Across the nation, programs began to develop rapidly. By the early and mid-1960's group counseling, usually of a Rogerian orientation, had spread to those correctional systems not earlier involved. In California in 1966, 14,000 to 16,000 offenders were involved in group counseling (Dunbar, 1966).

Arnold and Stiles (1972) report that a survey covering this period showed that the percentage of institutions using group methods increased from 35% in 1950, to 50% in 1959, to 70% in 1966. They caution, however, against over-interpretation of these data since, of the 70% of the institutions providing group treatment, one-fifth included fewer than 20% of the inmates. By the early 1970's, some correctional systems considerably experienced with this approach to counseling came to question its value. In turn, these systems started to explore new and different ways to modify the attitudes and feelings contributing to criminal behavior.

Settings for Counseling

Most of the literature on the subject of counseling offenders deals with counseling, group counseling, and some of the newer approaches as they apply in the prison setting. Good reasons for focusing on the prison setting are the concentration of inmates there, the ease of mobilizing professional help, and the strong feelings of the public that "something must be done." However, counseling of offenders takes place in other settings. For those not incarcerated but placed under the supervision of a probation officer, individual counseling has been a mainstay of the probationary concept since its inception. It is only recently and rather sporadically that group techniques or other methods have been introduced into probationary supervision. Some of the more innovative approaches will be examined in later sections of this paper. Although the parole activities parallel those in the area of probation, they have surprisingly selected quite different techniques.

Local jails probably represent one of the greatest wastelands in terms of providing a setting for treatment of any kind, particularly counseling. Many settings within the correctional system would be appropriate for counseling activities. These include diversionary programs, group homes for juvenile offenders, halfway houses, and juvenile and adult felony institutions.

There are also distinct differences between counseling clients at the local, state, and federal levels. Due to different statutes and jurisdictions, individuals involved in similar kinds of crimes are handled by different levels of government, and therefore receive different kinds and qualities of treatment.

Different Clients

Offenders are a very heterogeneous group who show more differences than similarities, and consequently have quite individual problems and needs. Counseling efforts have been distributed along a variety of dimensions in order to determine what kinds of programs might be most appropriate for different kinds of individuals. Counselors have attempted to deal with such groups as the pre-delinquent, the juvenile offender, the young adult offender, and the hardened criminal. Within these groups are also the subgroups of the alcoholic, the drug abuser, the sexual offender, and the emotionally disturbed. Offenders range from the truant to the murderer, the "peeping Tom" to the rapist, the kleptomaniac to the bank robber. There are some situations in which similar approaches are taken with all kinds of clients, and others in which different approaches are used to meet different kinds of problems. From the wide range of offenses and the multi-dimensional causal factors of crime, it can be seen that we are dealing with complex, many-faceted behaviors within an infinitely diverse client population. Obviously, no single type of treatment can be expected to work in all cases.

Different Approaches

Some techniques, such as certain types of behavior modification, can be applied only in one-to-one relationships. Other approaches can be either individual or group-oriented. Given the numbers of people subjected to the correctional process and the limited funds and personnel available, the emphasis tends to be consistently placed on group applications.

The aim of the program also determines what techniques will be most appropriate. Whether the aim is to modify either the internal variables or the observable behavior of the individual without regard to attitudinal shifts is important. Similarly, the values of counseling approaches that emphasize the study of personal historical developments versus "here and now" interaction will be explored.

Directive counseling versus client-centered counseling, lay or paraprofessional counseling versus professional counseling, small group versus therapeutic community are all areas that must be examined. This will result in a comprehensive understanding of the meaning and significance of the counseling programs being attempted throughout the total correctional spectrum.

Some Basic Assumptions

One of the most basic assumptions underlying all counseling efforts is that offenders can and do change in their approach to life. This may appear to be a self-evident truth to some. But the fact is that for many hundreds of years, offenders were identified as "criminal types" and, even as late as the early 1900's, drastic labels were employed that implied constitutional defects. These defects were believed to predispose an individual to crime to such an extent that any change in adjustment was impossible. Views that some individuals are "inherently bad," still persist among some correctional workers. We also see the same attitude on the part of psychiatric staff when they use the term "psychopathic personality," a label that has been erased from the nomenclature for 25 years. It was not too long ago that the diagnostic nomenclature definition for classifying this group included the idea that if the individual responded to treatment, he or she could not be a true psychopath. This logic remarkably is similar to that of the "dunking test" for witches in early American times.

At any rate, the treatment model of correctional practice now embraces the concept that most, if not all, inmates can respond to some sort of therapeutic or counseling intervention, which can bring about concomitant changes in behavior. In its formative stages, counseling developed from a psychotherapeutic base and therefore places considerable emphasis on "understanding" and "insight" as prerequisites for overt changes in behavior. Melitta Schneideberg describes this very well in her recent book (1974):

> There can be no cure without understanding. Psychotherapy must always be combined with other types of help and can only be effective against the background of social and legal justice (p. 137).

Freud's "talking cure," supplemented by Rogerian theories of nondirective counseling helped shape the methodology in corrections. The idea was that talking through problems deeply buried within the unconscious could bring them to consciousness and full understanding. With that accomplished, their crippling influence would be lessened and the individual would be free to function more appropriately. The belief that reducing interpsychic tension could bring relief from symptoms, although somewhat magical in nature, was held by many. This procedure, when achieved under therapeutic conditions, is labeled "insight." Other classic concepts of counseling including identification, defense mechanisms, id, ego, superego, libido, drive, and other Freudian and neo-Freudian concepts, relate internal dynamic structures to criminal behavior and incorporate these into the counseling model.

The transition from therapy to counseling was an attempt to give the client the opportunity to examine a variety of alternatives to a problem solution. As anyone who has worked with law violators will agree, many of these individuals are quite limited in their ability to adapt to different roles in life, and also to see the world from the other fellow's point of view. As a result, individuals apparently have adjustment difficulties when they try to adapt a single solution to a broad set of personal, social, and emotional problems. This, quite naturally, brings us to discuss the idea that counseling might assist in the battle against crime through the rehabilitation of offenders. Many would argue that while most offenders are not mentally ill, they are in need of basic counseling and positive social models.

Once the idea that offenders were some sort of "incurable monsters" was overcome, the next logical trap into which most people fell was that such individuals were "sick." They were characterized as being maladjusted, antisocial, and mentally ill, all psychiatric euphemisms for "bad." However, there was a strong belief that somehow people could be "corrected" by becoming "adjusted." They are subsequently ready for reentry into the mainstream of society in a positive manner.

Such an approach fitted neatly with the psychotherapeutic activities of the time that directed considerable efforts toward exploring the development underlying the "complexes" causing the observed problems. Later, disillusionment with this medical model started to develop for at least two observable reasons. The first of these was that a number of people seemed to develop an understanding of their problems without any change in behavior. The second was that even though some people developed this understanding *and* improved their behaviors while under direct supervision, they reverted to unlawful behavior when the supervision ceased.

The major problem here is that the basic assumption that offenders are "sick" has never been fully examined with any scientific rigor. In the first place, there is little or no solid evidence to support the notion that most violators are seriously emotionally disturbed, or emotionally disturbed at all. If we assume that a disturbed person is one who would require the services of a professional mental health worker in the community, then we would find only a very few who would qualify. Most surveys, however, in search of personality maladjustment tend to find it. A recent survey of the extent of serious emotional problems among prison inmates during various periods of times suggested that the key factor in determining this extent was the number of psychiatrists available to make such diagnoses rather than the maladjustments of the individual inmates involved (see Brodsky, 1973, pp. 61–67, for further discussion of the medical model).

Also contesting this basic assumption is the question whether or not violations of the law are actually expressions of emotional maladjustment. It seems both likely and possible for illegal behavior to occur as a fairly reasonable solution to various situational stresses. For the purpose of this paper, this question will remain essentially unanswered. But keeping it in mind will remind the readers that no matter how effective a psychotherapy or counseling program might be, it will be helpful for only a portion of the group for which it has been designed.

SUMMARY

Counseling in corrections has evolved from an essentially punitive orientation to a belief that offenders can learn new behaviors through supportive and positive kinds of activities. Because the individuals in the correctional system vary from predelinquents to hardened criminals, a wide variety of techniques and approaches is necessary for dealing with their problems and concerns. Counselors in this field believe strongly that in most cases offenders are not inherently bad or sick but are responding to internal and situational stresses with inappropriate behaviors. They also believe that offenders can and do change with help.

Chapter 2

APPROACHES TO COUNSELING IN THE CORRECTIONAL SETTING

Within this chapter attempts are made to examine in some detail various approaches taken in counseling offenders. There is also a brief exposition of the different theoretical orientations of each approach and of each one's implementation within the correctional setting.

INDIVIDUAL COUNSELING

The effectiveness of individual counseling in changing behavior or in reducing delinquent behaviors has never been adequately researched. One of the major disadvantages of individual counseling is the tremendous cost. The simple economic efficiency of the group approach probably accounts for its rapid acceleration across the nation. Despite whatever limitations may be identified, however, individual counseling remains a mainstay of much of the work within correctional systems. Consider, for example, the probationary system. To the extent that probation relies upon some sort of interpersonal relationship to change behavior, individual counseling is far and above the most common technique employed. Group procedures have been used in this field only sporadically.

While documentation is not readily available, the earliest efforts in the area of individual counseling probably tended to be authoritarian. Early efforts were more than likely to be mixed with religious exhortations, and later evolved to be more inspirational, cajoling kinds of efforts. In more recent years it may be assumed that these attempts moved to discussions of alternative modes of responding to problems and attempting to relate to offenders in an empathetic, accepting manner.

GROUP COUNSELING

The movement from individual counseling to group counseling probably stemmed more from economic conditions than from any theoretical rationale. Of course, theory is part of group counseling. Roberts (1972) noted that inasmuch as many theories about delinquent behavior involve the concept of peer pressure, group counseling aimed toward developing positive peer pressure can be theoretically supported.

Much has already been said or written about the economic advantages of group counseling. However, too often correctional administrators do not realize that group counseling is a *different kind* of treatment approach. The contributions of Slavson and Moreno were mentioned earlier. Another main influence was the National Training Laboratory's "sensitivity training" program. Social group work has also come to be an accepted activity within social work, and is a main component of graduate training in social work and psychology curricula.

The advantages of group counseling have to be more substantial than those of economics alone. As a matter of fact, group counseling is often doomed to failure if undertaken solely for economic reasons.

Groups can work well in correctional settings with open dormitory living quarters. Many of the activities in these settings involve groups, whether structured by staff or spontaneously formed by the residents. Inmate cliques can become very powerful unless group counseling opportunities are structured around resident needs and treatment goals within an institution. Cliques are often less healthy for individual growth and effective operation of the correctional facility. When left to offenders, groupings are often established along religious lines, home town associations ("homies"), offense partners ("rappies"), racial lines, and/or sexual habits ("fags"). These groupings can result in intragroup misunderstandings, unnecessary tension among residents, and breakdown of interaction with staff.

The advantages of group versus individual counseling are often debated, and many of the issues become clouded within the setting of the penal institution. The unique characteristics of the members of the group make group counseling a radically different treatment modality from individual counseling. Several major factors can be identified as being responsible for this difference.

First of all, the "inmate code" in youth and young adult institutions, and the "way of the con" in adult facilities do not allow for free expression with staff because it can so easily be construed as "snitching." As a result, residents are quite reluctant to express their opinions openly in group counseling situations. This behavior, coupled with a great hesitation to show feelings, makes group counseling in correctional institutions excessively difficult.

Offenders also want to appear "tough" to others in order to reduce their vulnerability to peer pressure in the institutional compound. Since residents will interpret a display of feelings as weakness, they will guard against any public show of emotion. Anyone who has ever been a correctional group counselor can easily attest to this reluctancy. An example of this occurred at the Federal Correctional Institution at Milan. While the leader was in the process of structuring a communications skills group, an inmate announced that he wanted to learn to communicate without involving his feelings, and if emotions were to be included, he would no longer participate in the group.

Another difficulty in conducting meaningful groups in correctional facilities is that the inmates may perceive them as threatening. The many male offenders who did not have an adequate male model early in life, may feel a basic insecurity regarding their own masculinity. Therefore, any threat to a resident's "manhood" such as a public display of feelings, or even joining a group, is to be shunned.

Manipulations and games are a given in the correctional setting. One common manipulation is the contention that a resident does not want anyone to know about his or her business. Therefore, he or she will talk about everything and say absolutely nothing. The ploy, as in most group situations, is to keep the conversation away from self and onto others or, preferably, general topics. Many qualified therapists have led discussion groups in prison settings without ever having any participant touch on the "self" or "I."

With all of these built-in barriers to group counseling in corrections, it becomes apparent that counselors must be truly dedicated to run meaningful groups. However, there is often mistrust and stereotyping on the part of the staff toward the inmates as there is on the part of the inmates toward the staff. In order to transcend this mutual negative feeling, both parties must take an open, honest approach. Developing openness takes time, patience, a sound understanding of the goals of the group, and the means for achieving these goals. Manipulations and games must be recognized and brought up for consideration. This takes experience not only in counseling techniques but also in working with offenders and dealing with them on a human level.

Several aspects of the group situation can be singled out as being important to and advantageous in the rehabilitation process. First, the group can be perceived as being very similar to the family. Playing such familiar roles within the group as expressing sibling rivalry or vying for the attention of the parent, can hopefully aid in developing understanding of one's place among others. This idea of family simulation can be carried too far, but often can serve as a conceptually sound way of expressing group dynamics.

Second, as documented in many sociology and social psychology texts, group problem-solving has definite advantages over individual solutions. The idea is that a wider variety of problem solutions can be elicited by drawing upon the experience of several people with varying backgrounds. Thus, one individual's problem may have already been solved by another, and the solution can be offered and applied. This notion that problem situations and their concomitant solutions can be generalized is crucial in the correctional milieu where so often the "inmate code" is to "do your own time." Such an attitude not only alienates inmates socially, but also results in distrust of others, suspicion, and possible loss of contact with reality. When a peer poses the solution, it often carries more weight, especially among socially alienated groups, than if the counselor (who is perceived as alien) were to suggest it.

This leads to the third advantage of group counseling, which has to do with identification and modeling. Bandura (1969) suggests conditions under which modeling can occur most readily, one of which is that a person can more readily model (that is, identify with) behaviors of individuals with attitudes, mores, background, and situations similar to his own. The identification and modeling concept, therefore, will be more pronounced in correctional settings than in the mental health field. Inmates, parolees, or probationers, with their distate for "The Man" or an unwritten moral "code," have a strong distrust for any advice or ideas presented by staff members. Almost every correctional worker at some time has been rebuffed by a retort such as, "How in the hell would you know what I am talking about

—you've never pulled any time." Since any trust these individuals feel seems to be based, in part, upon common experience, the group allows them to learn from people they trust.

One characteristic of most applications of group counseling in the correctional field is the broad array of staff people involved. Whereas psychotherapy requires a psychologist or psychiatrist or a highly trained social worker, it is felt that group counseling sessions can be conducted by almost any staff person who has a minimal amount of training. Thus, shop foremen, secretaries, and correctional officers, as well as the usual treatment staff, are often involved in and carry on the group counseling program. The Federal Bureau of Prisons has developed a new promotional direction for correctional officers that offers a counseling career for those so suited and motivated. Traditionally this opportunity did not exist, and an officer would advance up the custodial hierarchy, seldom having the opportunity for counseling relationships with offenders. Through counseling activities, correctional counselors have provided valuable liaison functions between staff and offenders. These counselors may be trained by the local institutions or the Bureau of Prisons in individual and group methods as designed by Carkhuff. This method of counseling will be described later (Truax, et al., 1966; Carkhuff and Truax, 1965).

Graduate students are also commonly employed as interns in the correctional facility. Together with the trained correctional professional and paraprofessional counselors, they usually contribute to a well-rounded counseling program in some of the more progressive state and federal facilities.

Within sociology, one of the major theories of delinquency concerns differential association (Cressey, 1955). This means that some people are forced to spend a great deal of time with undesirable companions, and that such association warps their thinking and social attitudes. Group counseling, group interaction, and other kinds of group activities can provide a corrective, positive experience that might help to offset the earlier delinquent association.

Another concept is "labeling." Within this process an individual involved in some sort of delinquent behavior becomes characterized in the eyes of others as "delinquent." Others react to the individual on the basis of this label, and thus he or she tends to behave in terms of what people believe about him or her. Group counseling or other counseling approaches can do little to mitigate the power of labeling, although understanding the behavior dynamics of such outside influences might enable one to maneuver more adroitly his or her personal adjustment.

Except in those approaches that require specific structure, prisoners are often left to decide for themselves how groups will be conducted. As will be seen later, this causes certain complications in evaluation. Some group leaders set up a small democratic community in which the group is encouraged to select a chairman, vote on topics, and delegate duties. Other leaders systematically rotate responsibilities for topics to be discussed at the next session. Still others operate a totally laissez-faire situation that goes beyond even the nondirective approach envisioned by Carl Rogers.

Four types of leaders emerged in a detailed study of a large number of groups in one California institution (Kassebaum, Ward and Wilner, 1963). The first was inhibiting, directing the discussion and laying out certain topics in order to keep the group on target. The second was stimulating, spending a great deal of time reflecting feelings and encouraging full, open participation. The third type of leader tended either to direct the gist of any discussion into nonthreatening channels or to deflect it. The fourth type was the authoritarian who favored action. If a certain problem were brought up for group discussion, she or he accepted the responsibility for trying to do something about the situation. The implication of this array is that one must be very careful in defining what is meant by "group counseling." Hanging a "Group Counseling Session" sign outside the door of the session room can signify a wide variety of activities.

A number of structured group approaches has emerged in the correctional field owing partly to the nature of the clientele and setting. One readily learns that there are two types of offenders who invariably become the focus of action within groups: the "manipulators" and the "controllers." Manipulation of the leader for desired ends is common in groups with older offenders. Among younger residents overt control—at times physical—is often attempted.

To avoid both types of subversion, a group counselor should structure his group carefully with clear-cut goals in mind. This may be done within the group using a consensus approach, or may be planned prior to initiating the group. As the traditional Rogerian approach may not lend itself to this type of structuring, new approaches may be needed. Appropriate choices will depend on the wisdom of experienced and well-trained group leaders.

At the Milan Federal Correctional Institution (FCI) at Milan, Michigan, case management personnel (social workers) and mental health staff (psychologists) have developed a number of methods to train staff in these structuring skills. One such method is Group Leadership Training as developed by Bertcher at The University of Michigan School of Social Work. This training is offered jointly to staff and inmates by means of thirteen structured two-hour sessions. It is aimed at developing specific skills which incorporate a number of counseling theories. From these sessions of readings, films, and exercises, the members actually initiate their own groups, building in the necessary structure to realize a successful experience.

At Milan FCI, group exercises as developed by NTL, Pfeiffer and Jones, Schutz, and others have been invaluable for developing a meaningful group experience for those involved.

Another method of structuring groups reduces the possible negative effects of offenders being left to their own controlling devices. Within this structure, the treatment or counseling target for the group is specified. From this functional model, focused efforts emerge such as drug groups, vocational counseling groups, alcoholics groups, communication skills groups, marriage counseling groups, and parent-child communication groups. These categories assemble offenders with common functional problems, and in effect help to create a natural cohesion within the group. Bringing in ex-drug addicts, ex-alcoholics, and ex-offenders to become part of the group often enhances this effect. Resident co-leaders also can contribute meaningful input into these groups.

Despite all of the ways there are of structuring a group, a counselor in corrections may frequently have to settle for what the inmates call a "rap" session. Here the main positive interaction is simply getting together once a week for conversation which many offenders find more desirable than doing their institutional work assignment. Even at this simplistic level, it is better than leaving the residents to group themselves.

CLIENT-CENTERED COUNSELING

One of the most powerful influences in counseling was the emergence in the 40's and 50's of Rogers' (1942) client-centered or nondirective counseling. Basic to this theory is the belief that counseling techniques could be learned in a reasonably short period of time, and that clients could gain insight into their own emotional hangups by listening to appropriate reflections of their feelings. While the approach was developed for college counseling and for dealing with mental health problems, it quickly was adopted for use in correctional settings. The ease of application, the common sense principles, and the occasional almost miraculous change in a client's outlook soon made the nondirective approach the model for much of correctional counseling. This approach was used with both individuals and groups in a variety of settings, including probation, incarceration, and parole.

To the students of Rogers, the idea of unconditional positive regard is almost a byword. Truax and Carkhuff (1965, 1967) scientifically explored the effects of nondirective counseling relative to subsequent emotional change developed through training programs, understanding, and *action*. They found that empathy, respect, and concern are necessary conditions for the development of understanding, out of which can then come some kind of directed action. In addition, having established a half dozen or so elements essential to counseling interaction to insure positive outcome, Carkhuff (1968) has developed an extensive system for training personnel in the helping professions. This system is extensively used in the Federal Bureau of Prisons and in state facilities.

TRANSACTIONAL ANALYSIS

Of more recent origin, Transactional Analysis (TA) has come to assume a major role in counseling within the correctional setting. Transactional Analysis, developed by Eric Berne in 1961 (modified by Tom Harris in 1969), has been acknowledged as an effective tool in correctional therapy by Frank Ernst (1962). After enjoying an initial period of high activity in California, Transactional Analysis tapered off. In recent years, however, it has reentered prominence, particularly in the federal system, in the form of peer counseling, which will be discussed in greater detail later.

At first glance, Transactional Analysis seems to be a popularized version of Freudian psychoanalysis. The *parent, adult,* and *child* seem to parallel the *superego, ego,* and *id.* It is only after considerable training and experience in working with the process that it becomes clear that Berne and Harris are talking about ego states that are readily accessible to conscious control, not unconscious constructs. Again, the technique was designed for psychotherapeutic interventions on a broader scale before it became subsequently incorporated into treatment approaches in the correctional field. Its advantage, which parallels the Rogerian approach, was the relative ease with which lay people could be trained in the new technique. The theory was well-structured and relatively easy to understand and to apply. The theoretical approach gave clients a real opportunity to develop a useful vocabulary to describe the processes that they experienced, which previously had often been difficult to put into words.

While Rogerian approaches take into consideration the relationship of the individual to those around him, the emphasis is largely upon the difficulties centering within the person. In contrast, Transactional Analysis, while legitimately applied to individual counseling, places heavy emphasis upon interactions among various individuals. Thus it, too, has quickly translated itself into a group approach.

Wichs (1974) comments that use of TA with offenders contributes much to treatment on several different fronts. TA explores the games that both offenders and staff play to hinder rehabilitation. One game Groder (1971) points out is "KUID" ("Keep It Up, Doc"). Here the therapist surrounds himself with patients who can be counted on to support him, even when he is ineffectual.

TA has adapted itself well to the correctional setting

by pointing out this and other games that interfere with meaningful change. "Games" permeate many staff-resident interactions, and are often used as a ploy by both to keep distance from one another. The idea is that neither inmates nor staff are sincere in their relationships. Staff's game is to look "good," to feel helpful, and to gain advancement. The offender only plays the game to gain earlier release, leaving avoidance of each other as the simplest solution. Rather than becoming "game-wise" through these interactions, the residents and staff become "game-shy" and never transcend this level of interaction. TA overcomes this by supplying a common language, understandable to both resident and staff, which leads to insight couched within the terminology of the methodology. Once the language is mastered, understanding replaces fear and avoidance on both fronts.

REALITY THERAPY

Reality Therapy (Glasser, 1965) does not distinguish between individual or group approaches. The emphasis in Glasser's model is to avoid elaborate discussions on the causes of behavior and center instead upon the behavior itself. Glasser recommends the use of Reality Therapy in the treatment of juvenile delinquents, and used it successfully in treating delinquent girls at Ventura School for Girls in California. It is his contention that the more psychoanalytically oriented therapies tend to provide offenders, particularly youthful offenders, with "excuses" for their misdeeds. According to Glasser, it is important that every individual face squarely his failures, gracefully accept the punishment due, and attempt to start off in more responsible and constructive directions. Glasser identifies two basic needs—the need to love and to be loved, and the need to feel that one is worthwhile to himself and others.

Helping patients to fulfill these needs is the basis of Reality Therapy. To achieve this, the therapist becomes actively emotionally involved with the client, rejecting his or her unrealistic, irresponsible behavior. At the same time the therapist teaches the client better ways to meet these needs within the bounds of reality.

In the case of psychoanalytically oriented psychotherapy and in Rogerian counseling, the counselor assumes a quiescent role, allowing the client to project upon him or her the distortions associated with parental or other early authority figures. In contrast, Reality Therapy suggests that the counselor share frankly with the client his or her experiences in life, pointing out the values of particular achievements and techniques of adaptation. The therapy gained rapid momentum because it matched so well with "common sense." It also fulfills to some extent the need for expressing the punitive feelings of society.

Reality Therapy has enjoyed a good deal of activity in group application. When used in juvenile halls and reformatories, it can become warped to justify a rather punitive, heavily disciplined approach to maintaining a quasi-military condition. When appropriately applied, however, this method can serve as a valuable tool for encouraging responsibility on the part of offenders.

GESTALT THERAPY

Gestalt therapy (Fritz Perls, 1951) is fairly new on the scene, and its application is somewhat limited. Part of the reason that Gestalt therapy has not spread more extensively in the correctional setting is its abstract theoretical foundation and the difficulty in training counselors in its use. The basic assumption is that mind and body are not separate, but rather a single entity, and thus we must "tune in" and integrate our totality. The techniques for achieving self-understanding through this process vary greatly, including such processes as sensory awareness exercises (subjective reporting of sensations while one takes the form of inanimate objects) and highly emotional encounter sessions.

Gestalt therapy techniques require a strong background in psychodynamics, and a willingness on the part of the therapist for total involvement with the group. This modality lends itself very well to offenders due to its focus on the "here and now" often expressed by offenders. Also, its existential underpinnings fit well with the prevalent pessimism and the feeling that life has no meaning. Gestalt allows persons to experientially "own" their projections, a helpful device for shifting an individual's perceived locus of control from external to internal. This approach, like Reality Therapy, encourages one to take responsibility for one's own feelings, behaviors, and their consequences. The common rationalization of offenders that society is out to get them can often change to a sincere awareness of their own responsibility in their dilemma. Again, it must be mentioned that Gestalt, as well as other emotionally-laden approaches, is quite difficult to use successfully due to the reality of the prison experience. In free society persons in therapy groups return to their homes and families and can get away from other group members. But in correctional settings group members often live together in a cell or dormitory. Therefore, caution should always be taken that closure is reached within the group and that unfinished business is not carried out into the general prison setting.

Behavior Modification

One of the newer techniques in the area of counseling is behavioral modification. Hosford and Moss (1973) state the theory quite succinctly:

> ... (the behavioral) view ... is that anti-social (i.e., criminal) behaviors are learned in the *same* way socially acceptable behaviors are ... This conceptualization ... has several implications ... It implies that behaviors ... are acquired through experience ... and as such can be altered by changing the contingencies which maintain and control that behavior (p. 91).

Unfortunately, some people think of electroshock therapy whenever behavior modification is mentioned. Those with a broader perspective may think of positive reinforcement in terms of tokens, payments, or gold stars. As far back as the early 1800's when convicts were transported to Australia, Maconochie established the basis for what is now characterized as a token or point economy. Maconochie's approach involved the following steps: 1) earned marks could be exchanged for extra food and luxuries, or to "purchase one's way out of prison;" 2) prisoners had to earn everything but the barest necessities; and 3) set tasks were not linked with time (Barry, 1965).

Such techniques do fit under the heading of behavior modification. However, there is a whole array of techniques regularly applied in counseling or psychotherapeutic activities that are only tangentially recognized, if at all, as behavior modification. For example, there is the Greenspoon Effect, wherein nonverbal or minimally verbal reinforcers are applied to the desired behavior. Suppose, for example, that one wishes to assist the client in reducing his or her use of obscenities. In individual sessions, whenever a string of epithets seems about to be emitted, the counselor turns slightly in the chair in such a way as almost to turn his back on the client. This motion would apply negative reinforcement. In contrast, while normal and constructive conversation is being carried out, the counselor would be in a posture evidencing excited interest. Careful recording of such procedures almost universally demonstrates that the undesired behavior will decrease and desired behavior will increase.

Another aspect of behavior modification is systematic desensitization. Wolpe (1969) based his work upon the psychological learning principle of reciprocal inhibition, a situation in which incompatible activities cannot be carried out simultaneously. The procedure helps the individual reduce the tensions of threatening circumstances by making him or her re-enact them in fantasy. For example, an individual might become quite emotionally tense and incapacitated when approaching an employer about a job. After a series of situations surrounding job application are discussed with the individual, the various scenes are arranged in a hierarchy from the least threatening to the most. By means of special training, the individual is taught how to reach a fairly complete state of emotional relaxation, at which time the least threatening situation is introduced in fantasy. The fantasy re-enactment is repeated until *all* tension is dissipated. Then the next most threatening situation is introduced. This procedure is carried out over time until the *most* threatening is re-enacted in fantasy to the point where it no longer carries an emotional threat. A parallel has been shown to exist between the loss of tension in the fantasy situation and the ability to handle that same situation in real life.

Within institutional settings operant conditioning procedures have been used to reinforce certain behaviors and to extinguish others. For the purpose of rewards, many target behaviors can be identified such as school attendance, being on time, creative endeavors, program participation, sociability, obedience, even attendance at the counseling sessions. On the other hand, anti-social activities such as refusal to participate in programs, and fighting can be punished. The rewards include such powerful motivators as remission in sentence, early parole, determination of parole in an indeterminate sentence, furloughs, town trips, promotions, wage increases, and tokens. Similarly, the punishment can be a loss, denial, demotion, forfeiture, or segregation. Quite obviously, if these rewards and punishments are used appropriately, correctional workers can influence greatly the inmates' behavior. However, these techniques become coercion and bribery when arbitrarily used, and are then only partially successful in inmate control. It takes only a short time in one of our prisons to realize how readily the system of control adapts to the language used by the behaviorists, and the techniques are by no means new. What is novel is their systematic application tied to evaluative research and carried out by qualified professional workers.

The application of behavior modification in group settings probably goes beyond the usual definition of group counseling. Almost everyone is aware of token economies to encourage training, academic achievement, conforming behavior, and changes in attitude. While the opponents of such programs characterize these activities as "bribery" or "brainwashing," similar types of programs have been employed throughout correctional history with the effects of incarceration itself being an important influence.

Token or point economies present unique problems to the correctional setting that make them difficult to initiate and follow through. A recent public outcry degrades "behavior modification" as an inhumane system designed to reduce human existence to the mechanistic. While we are all motivated by rewards and punishment, behavior modification is more of a danger to the offender in the correctional system than to the citizen of a free society. When applied to individuals who are confined in a limited space and highly motivated to leave that space, this therapy must be done carefully, in a humanistic manner, and in a spirit of benefitting rather than merely controlling offenders.

This does not call for abandoning effective behavioral techniques in these settings, but for educating those using these approaches. By merely stating to offenders, "If you do this, then I will give you that," the correctional worker can go beyond effectively controlling inmates to also shape desirable behaviors that lead to societal adjustment. Writing behavioral contracts with offenders and using a goal sheet in inmate classification can do much to clarify expectancies so that the result of confinement can be accomplishment. This is preferable to a vague sense of "What do I have to do?" expressed by residents and staff. The goals are clearly defined and the accomplishments are easy to see.

It seems possible to treat the offenders humanely, while segregating them from society, and still serve a deterrent function. It is further maintained that an educated, well-meaning behavioral approach can be a valuable tool in achieving this balance. We must approach the techniques rationally and answer those we serve, both offenders and public, regarding rationale and methodology.

FAMILY COUNSELING

This approach views the individual offender as part of a social network in which the family plays a leading role, and which facilitates his or her adjustment and maladjustment. Those working in a correctional setting often witness the tremendous strain that an individual undergoes as she or he moves back into the intimate relationships within the family. The counseling program attempts to involve not only the spouse of the incarcerated individual but the children as well, since they all play a part in the acceptance of the offender into society and probably will influence his subsequent adjustment to a significant degree.

Dramatic illustrations of the effect that family counseling can bring about have occurred in the California family visit program. Families, including children, are permitted to visit and live with the offender in a small apartment for a period of three days and two nights. One wife reported that her husband paced the floor on the first night, and she concluded that he was feeling totally alien in the new environment. She noted that this behavior was remarkably similar to the behavior he showed the first night at home following an earlier release from prison to parole. Bringing this conclusion to his attention and discussing it to some extent helped to develop considerable understanding between the husband and wife. Earlier, the wife had erroneously assumed that her husband's strange behavior indicated a lack of affection for her. Because of this misperception about his motivation, she reacted negatively. This led the husband to feel more and more alienated and rejected, and subsequently led to his parole violation. It is just such problems that can be worked through in family counseling to help stave off the future development of behavior problems.

Family counseling very likely will represent one of the more rapidly developing areas of counseling in the correctional setting as the emphasis on community-based programs gains full momentum. This is not a *new* program, but rather one that has suffered setbacks in its development, largely because institutions are usually remote from population centers, making interaction between the inmate and his or her family extremely difficult.

At the Milan Federal Correctional Institution, a Family Unit exists that accepts only married offenders. The unit programs evolve around structured groups designed for parent training, marital counseling, and communications skills training. Where possible, efforts are made to keep the family intact and to involve the wife and children in counseling the offender. The idea of a man's returning to his family after incarceration is strongly supported throughout the entire federal prison system. Research has shown that "blood is thicker than water," at least for parolees. Residents are therefore counseled to reestablish family ties upon release, and location of release is usually an individual's hometown.

In 1961, to reduce the alienating effect of returning from prison to the community and family, the Federal Bureau of Prisons established a network of Community Program centers (CPC). These halfway house CPC's provide counseling, job placement, and live-in support for offenders who previously would have been thrust after total institutionalization into an alien situation. These centers are often contract facilities operated by state, local and private establishments as well by the federal government. It also must be mentioned that a significant percentage of adult offenders have no family ties, which is often an indication that most program efforts are doomed to failure.

LARGE GROUP INTERACTION (COMMUNITY LIVING GROUPS)

Two specific modalities are being applied now in the correctional setting to make better use of both professional and paraprofessional staff; one is therapeutic community (TC), and the other is guided group interaction (Wichs, 1964).

Following World War II a British psychiatrist, Maxwell Jones (1953), believed that a number of people in mental hospitals did not really belong there and that the services provided for them did not meet their needs. Jones observed that doctors made only limited, sporadic individual contacts. Likewise, nurses performed their duties in "stations" and acted in a prescribed authoritarian manner. Jones felt that if staff acted more like people than professionals, it might motivate these marginally adjusted clients to function more effectively. He also believed that patients could be useful to each other. Thus, he developed a system of ward management that became known as the "therapeutic community." This approach involves learning through experiencing a healthy human interaction between staff and inmates, accessibility of professionals, and mutual problem-solving.

The theoretical basis for the therapeutic community has not been well defined. One concept has to do with the group's "holding a mirror up to the individual." This point of view can be nicely meshed with that of social group work previously mentioned:

> Human beings can be understood only in relation to other human beings. What a man is, is reflected in the views of other men toward him. What a man thinks of himself is his judgment of the reaction of other men, too. The behavior pattern of any individual is a mirror of his total life experience, most of which is in groups. If one is to understand an individual, one must know the groups to which he belongs. Every individual has a different status in each of the variety of groups to which he belongs. The same individual will exhibit different patterns of behavior in different groups (Wilson and Ryland, 1949).

Many of the groups focus on current problems of living together. Thus, in institutional settings, even towel exchanges or bunk assignments are items for lengthy analysis. Disciplinary problems aired in the group setting combine peer pressure toward conformity with a clear examination of the emotional components in most human interactions. Many such groups insist upon examining only "here and now" interactions. They vehemently eschew any tendency of the group to examine historical antecedents or early childhood occurrences that might account for present day behaviors. Historical causality or diagnostic labeling is considered noncontributory.

Although 12 is considered to be the maximum number

of participants for effective group learning, the group size tends to range between 10 and 60 people.

In the TC, approaches ranging from psychoanalysis to behavior modification may be employed. However, the emphasis is usually on social activities that involve group dynamics, environmental examination, and improvement of communications. The TC was not applied extensively in the penal setting until the 60's. One of the earliest in-depth studies was carried out between 1964 and 1966 at the NIMH Research Center in Texas. It involved 30 drug addicts, prisoners who were found to be particularly resistant to traditional therapy. The residents had developed cliques based on negative reactions to certain staff members. To change this situation, staff decided to give inmates responsibilities, such as discipline, traditionally held by staff. Inmates and staff also began to participate together in community meetings. The results of the study showed that these changes enhanced communication between staff and inmates, markedly improving the TC's rehabilitative program (Hughes, 1970). Other studies of TC programs include The Clinton Study (Efthihiades and Fink, 1968) and The Patuxent Institution Study (Wilson and Snodgrass, 1969). This technique can be applied to a wide variety of settings, but is most often used in halfway houses operated by self-help groups.

Guided Group Interaction (GGI) was initially used with youthful offenders in a halfway house in the "Highfields Project" in New Jersey (McCorkle, 1958). The success of the Highfields Project led to others such as Walton Village (Montone, 1967) and the Florida and Minnesota corrections systems (Larson, 1970). The President's Commission on Law Enforcement and Administration of Justice reported that in terms of time and cost the GGI approach at Highfields achieved positive results more effectively and efficiently than do most reformatories (President's Commission, 1967).

Other Approaches

Kanfer and Saslow (1969) do not limit their analysis of individual problems to excesses, deficits, and assets. They also discuss the extent of the individual's self-control, the quality of his/her social relationships, and the entire supportive environment in which the individual is operating. Bandura (1969) emphasizes "social modeling" as one of the systems through which people can learn and subsequently change.

New techniques are emerging in the area of assertive training. Here the underlying assumption is that many offenders exhibit illegal behavior because of their inability to confront directly any emotionally threatening situation. Techniques range from specific instructions concerning ways to become more assertive, to modeling and role-playing, to behavioral rehearsal. Since these approaches show a movement away from simply "talking" as an attempt to understand behavior toward becoming involved in action, they represent a shift from traditional counseling techniques. Little concern may be given to whether the individual understands the dynamics of the change, and the methodology for achieving positive change is directed toward new habit formation.

Despite its negative reputation in some circles, behavior modification provides a strong positive aspect in that it approaches problems differently and is markedly more effective than the traditional punishment model. In this framework, punishment is seen as an attempt to extinguish a certain type of behavior. Studies in this area indicate that for punishment to be effective in deterring behaviors, the aversive stimuli must be applied within seconds after the undesired behavior occurs, with enough severity to eliminate the behavior. This immediacy is next to impossible in a correctional setting. Another disadvantage of the punishment model is that it increases such emotions as anger and fear, which interfere with learning. If the offenders are to learn more adaptive behaviors, it is self-defeating to use approaches that reduce the chances of learning. From a psychological point of view, this brief analysis shows that the likelihood of such a procedure being effective is quite remote, given the inexactness with which it is likely to be applied in the correctional setting and the detrimental effects associated with this approach.

Positive reinforcement, on the other hand, can be effectively applied within the behavioral modification framework. In this procedure, a systematic attempt is made to reward or reinforce positive behaviors and ignore negative behaviors. This results in an increase in the likelihood that the rewarded behaviors will occur in the future. This model obviously poses problems within the correctional setting. Many negative behaviors are difficult or impossible to ignore, especially when they involve the well-being of other individuals. Other ill effects are further criminal prosecution, such as use of illicit drugs in prison, assaults, and even occasional killings. These facts do not preclude, though, attempts to design positive reinforcement programs directed toward specific goals for individual offenders or groups of offenders.

By using positive reinforcement techniques, records of change or nonchange in the target behaviors can be accumulated leading to an accurate assessment of the effects of the program. As many of the earlier counseling approaches either can not or do not identify clearly treatment objectives, it is impossible to measure their results or to present statistical evidence of the efficacy of the approach.

Many correctional workers find it difficult to incorporate the nonpunishment model into their thinking because it runs counter to two general public mandates of correctional facilities—those of deterrence and retribution. In direct contrast to these traditional mandates are the concepts of rehabilitation and provision of a humane environment for persons forcibly removed from society. These vastly different approaches continually conflict for those responsible for both the treatment and custodial aspects of corrections.

In addition to this conflict, positive reinforcement programs can present problems in correctional settings if they are inappropriately applied by poorly trained staff. For example, it is quite easy to withdraw rights and privileges within a contained environment. When misused in this manner, these reinforcers can have the reverse effect of creating more negative than positive feelings in the residents. In some mental hospitals basic bedding is removed and is returned only on the basis of the patients' displaying the desired behaviors. This raises a question about the motivations of correctional personnel. Who are we helping? Very often it is only the institution or ourselves.

Other emerging approaches in counseling include the use of biofeedback techniques, hypnotherapy, and meditative procedures which hold much promise for dealing with such problems as reducing anxiety or rehabilitating drug offenders. Biofeedback techniques have been applied in the Federal Correctional Facility at Lompoc, California, and Transcendental Meditation was successfully used with a group of drug offenders at the Milan Michigan Federal Correctional Institute (Ramirey, 1975).

Other counseling and therapy modalities that have gained some prominence in correctional work include Offender Therapy as practiced by the Association for the Psychiatric Treatment of Offenders, Rationale-Emotive Therapy of Albert Ellis (1961), Logotherapy, and Crisis Therapy.

SUMMARY

Counseling approaches in corrections vary widely and encompass techniques commonly used in other kinds of counseling situations. Although it presents unique problems in the correctional setting, group counseling is practiced in a variety of formats, depending upon the focus of the counseling efforts. Family counseling is conceived to be important and necessary to rehabilitating offenders, and community living groups are now being organized among offenders to provide real-life settings for acquiring and practicing more appropriate social behaviors. Many new techniques are on the horizon, and their efficacy is yet to be assessed.

Chapter 3

DIFFERING OBJECTIVES

This chapter discusses differing objectives that may be achieved through three major kinds of programmatic efforts: career guidance, general adjustment, and emotional reorientation. Ways of tailoring these objectives to individual client needs are also discussed.

Discussing which of the widely differing approaches will be most appropriate for correctional counseling will often depend on the intent of the counseling effort. Counseling activities can range from direct advice-giving, through a variety of role-playing and behavior analyses, to intensive interpretations of a psychotherapeutic nature. One way to determine appropriateness might be to assess the *depth* of involvement expected from the participant. At one end of the continuum, that of advice giving, we expect the individual to be rather superficially involved. She or he is expected to be psychologically adjusted only to the point where she or he can make intelligent choices among alternatives. His or her emotional investment is likely to be limited, and she or he is expected to respond with the conscious mind in terms of an adequately functioning ego—in TA terms, as an "adult."

At the other end of the continuum, the counseling program attempts to involve the individual more deeply, bringing emotions clearly into focus so they can be examined by the individual, and often by the group. The aim is for the individual to achieve "insight" or some similar type of improved understanding of his or her own motivational pattern. In the following pages the differing objectives are discussed under the three headings of career guidance, general adjustment, and emotional reorientation.

Career Guidance

One example of direct application of factual information is career counseling, including rehabilitation guidance. In correctional institutions across the nation, counselors are on hand to insure that inmates understand what programs are being offered, the employment possibilities associated with training activities, and the value and importance of education. These persons may be called educational counselors, vocational counselors, and/or rehabilitation counselors, and they provide information in different, but interrelated, areas. In other settings, the three functional counseling areas may be combined into one, and is conducted under the heading of "career guidance," providing not only occupational information but also discussion of values and attitudes.

The purpose of career guidance is to provide the client with information about the kinds of programs available to him or her, how the particular program is related to the labor market in the free community, and how available opportunities would tie into further developmental activities following institutional release. Counseling sessions usually orient the individual to reality and exhort him or her to accept and adapt to middle class mores, including the virtue of the work ethic. Graduate students often work in career guidance programs in the fields of vocational rehabilitation, guidance and counseling, social work, and related disciplines. They are especially helpful with young adults, who find it easier to identify with staff closer to their own ages.

Along with providing information about opportunities, procedures include analyzing the individual's strengths and weaknesses in terms of aptitudes, interests, and capabilities. The inmate is allowed time to realistically assess his or her potential for completing the course. On a longer range basis the individual can make the decision to work in the field if the course requirements are satisfactorily completed. Little emphasis is placed on emotional aspects of the choices being made. Career counseling is designed for people who are capable of functioning adequately and are essentially free from serious emotional maladjustment.

Vocational rehabilitation programs are emerging more frequently in institution and in probationary and parole operations. Part of the trend seems to be based on the concept that behavior and personality disorders represent disabilities of a severity equal to some kinds of physical incapacitation. State departments of vocational rehabilitation have become actively involved in correctional settings and offer their support and services when emotional and physical disabilities interfere with the offender's ability to function independently in the job market.

Career counseling also is a part of the normal procedure of both probation and parole supervision. The conditions of release under supervision almost inevitably include some requirement to maintain gainful employment, or in the case of more youthful offenders, to be actively involved in school or skills training. If individuals are to adjust in the community, they often need considerable assistance in reorganizing their lives, particularly in fulfilling work obligations. They need practical counseling on such subjects as the availability of financial support for vocational training, opportunities for training or education, and available job opportunities. Because many correctional workers and inmates are unaware that there are job opportunities in many states that are closed to ex-offenders, they must be made known in reality-based counseling.

Another trend within the correctional picture involving fairly directive counseling is the self-help group efforts. Offenders are trained as paraprofessionals to assist their peers with making use of both the support bureaucracy and employment and training resources available to them.

General Adjustments

Somewhere between advice-giving and in-depth psychotherapy lie many counseling activities, which are concerned with assisting individuals to function more productively in society rather than with psycho-dynamic emotional adjustment.

Within this framework are such approaches as the TC and GGI, communication skills groups, Alcoholics Anonymous, drug information groups, and self-help groups. The goals of many of these groups are to provide information and promote interaction leading to more effective social adjustment. The efforts of the counselor are directed toward creating an environment wherein this effect may be optimally realized. To this end the groups are usually democratically organized, with maximum inmate input, and relatively free from autocratic staff participation.

One promising approach is Group Leadership Training, briefly discussed in Chapter 2. This procedure opens the door for future inmate-led groups with self-determined goals and objectives. Granted, all the solutions presented are not necessarily related to the needs of *all* individuals participating. Rather, individual participants make use of those aspects of the program seen as most beneficial to themselves. Although not entirely successful for many people going through the correctional process, such programs have served as a turning point in the lives of some individuals, leading to social adjustment and other achievements.

A general adjustment approach can often prove beneficial for individuals with fairly severe emotional problems. Recovery, Inc., for example, founded by Dr. Abraham Low, was based upon very practical guides for living to be taught to and practiced by former mental patients. Techniques employed parallel the Schmidhofer technique (1973) in some respects. This latter approach teaches specific skills to large groups of individuals. Students do not discuss their emotional difficulties but share their experiences with the prescribed techniques to overcome some problem. Dr. Schmidhofer used this procedure in several correctional settings with mixed results. For many, a generalized program missed the mark. For a selected few, considerable gains could be observed.

While many of the self-help group efforts tend to be planned approaches toward social adjustment, they often develop a psychotherapeutic orientation and deal with emotions as well. Programs such as Synanon and Peer Counseling use a very structured approach incorporating therapeutic techniques like TA and Gestalt.

One argument against many general adjustment approaches within an institutional setting is that they provide skills necessary for institutional adjustment but not for living in a free society. This problem can be resolved only by providing an institutional environment closer to normal society, which may involve vast systems change. Much systems change has come about as the direct result of new needs for staff and residents created by the general adjustment approach. The Federal Bureau of Prisons has recently initiated a management restructuring program aimed at normalizing the correctional setting.

The unit management system allows for more effective TC's, GGI's, and other adjustment programs because it not only focuses on normalization, but, by decentralizing institution staff into units, it also places staff with decision-making authority in close proximity to the offenders. This encourages increased staff-inmate interaction and the restructuring of inmate cliques into adjustment oriented groups.

EMOTIONAL REORIENTATION

While most counseling efforts avoid committing themselves to psychodynamic objectives, many group leaders still strive to achieve some measure of personality reorganization in the participants.

One aspect of emotional reorientation concerns developing a more flexible adaptability to life. Close examination reveals that, from the point of view of the individual, becoming involved in illegal, antisocial acts represented almost the only possible solution to a complex dilemma. Only after exhaustive exploration of motivations and emotional blockages can the individual come to understand that a number of alternatives would be available in future situations. The statement is often heard that, "If I had only stopped to think about it, I would have never done it." Indeed, this may very well be true. It is not unusual for individuals to allow pressures to accumulate until the motivations forcing them toward certain types of actions are beyond recognition. They then react impulsively. Thus, a variety of techinques in the therapeutic approach assists individuals to understand their own dynamic processes and helps them to analyze why they are behaving as they do. They are also encouraged to explore the extent to which they can exercise control over their own behavior, and integrate their cognitive and emotional lives.

For example, in Transactional Analysis, understanding the different ego states and how a person shifts from one to another lead to developing understanding of the motivations for one's own behavior and how certain types of reactions are triggered. The "60-Second Countdown" technique provides for short-term analysis of social interaction, quickly shifting the individual into the analytic mode for a more reasoned response.

Similarly, the "here and now" group feedback process, centering on expressing emotions, can "hold up the mirror" to an individual so that he can see himself as others see him. Role-playing, modeling, and identification are all processes that are used in most therapy sessions toward an improved degree of emotional reorientation.

While behavior modification techniques appear to be more closely related to the "general adjustment" approach to counseling, the fact of the matter is that they are often in the emotional reorientation framework. Counseling efforts growing out of the older psychoanalytic approach and Rogerian type counseling emphasize that "understanding" and "insight" of underlying emotional motivations must precede behavior change. On the other hand, supporters of behavior modification contend that it is considerably more efficient to approach the problem in reverse —namely, change the behavior and the associated emotions will subsequently change. Thus, as the individual becomes free from anxiety and tension through systematic desensitization, he enjoys greater success in tackling problems. As a result, the individual develops a more success-oriented emotional outlook.

Assertive training is an even better example of the alliance between behavior modification and emotional reorientation. Here, through changing a behavior pattern, the individual learns how to function more adequately. In the process, of course, she or he also discovers the basis for problems in this area in the past. This latter insight is of less consequence than the very positive feelings the individual has in moving toward more adequate functioning and finds others reacting toward him or her in more satisfying ways.

It is often quite difficult to achieve emotional reorientation in the correctional setting. The combined factors of a coercive atmosphere, conflicting treatment mandates, and the "inmate code" act against the success of traditional modes of psychotherapy. One solution is to request professional persons outside the correctional system to administer these services. This is an expensive procedure, requiring care in employing consultants and in choosing resident participants. Very often inmates, who are neither motivated to seek out psychotherapy nor in need of an intensive emotional growth experience, are attracted to therapy programs rich in community consulting staff as they provide situations where their privileges can be extended and their release more rapidly effected.

One example of this occurred at the Milan FCI in the early 70's, where a treatment community of "disturbed" offenders was established. Preferential housing was furnished, the staff was buttressed with community professional consultants and most of the institution's mental health professionals. This island of treatment and privileges within a custodially-oriented correctional setting created discord among inmates and staff alike. The inmate population in the unit, consisting of the most dominant-athletic residents at the time, was dissolved. It appeared that those inmates who were the most vocal and persistent gained admission to the unit. A mixture of these residents with the "disturbed" label finally culminated in a privilege unit that was operating for reasons far different from those for which it was designed.

Care must always be taken to set policies and programs in such a way that treatment objectives do not interfere with basic overall procedures. Conflict may result in more problems than can be solved through the treatment process. Consultants, staff professionals, and students can effectively design and operate therapy programs, especially when the entire institution can benefit equally from this expertise.

Judge David L. Bazelon, a Federal Judge from the Washington, D.C. District, has argued that psychologists' treatment programs have served mainly as a side show that distracts from the main ring—societal reorganization. He maintains that psychologists have served themselves well, but not the offenders they are asked to help (Brodsky, 1973). In talking to psychologists he states:

> "... you may find that you can have a significant impact on the problem of violent crime by taking bitter and violent offenders and reshaping them so that they learn to live with the devastating and ugly conditions of life that none of us could tolerate ... But whether you want to serve as high-priced janitors who sweep up society's debris so that our problems will be pushed out of sight but in no sense resolved, is a question that you yourselves must answer after you have squarely faced it."

DIFFERING CLIENTS

In an attempt to deal with each person as an individual a great amount of energy is devoted to diagnosing each one's unique problems. But the fact of the matter is that the resulting prescription is often remarkably similar across clients—namely, group counseling, or whatever. This is not to imply that a special counseling program should be specifically designed for each individual and his special problem, but rather that clients may be grouped according to their major presenting problem, and perhaps, unique approaches developed to deal with those problems.

A form of this latter approach seems to be emerging already. Many states and the federal government have initiated "special treatment" programs for those having a history of narcotic addiction. Jurisdictions have developed specialized programs for people with such problems within the existing institutional settings. Similarly, those with problems of alcohol abuse separate themselves out for special attention. For many years Alcoholics Anonymous was about the only treatment modality available in either the mental hospital or prison setting other than Antibuse. Recently, specialized counseling programs have been initiated for this group. As has been previously indicated, youthful offenders are often provided with a wider range of treatment opportunities.

Summary

Career guidance programs focus on imparting factual information about the kinds of programs being offered, employment possibilities, and the value of education. General adjustment programs aim at teaching skills necessary for living in a free society. To that end attempts are being made to make institutions resemble more closely the normal societal milieu. More difficult to implement than the foregoing are programs for emotional or personality reorientation, although many programs will include some efforts in this area. In designing any program for a correctional setting, caution must always be taken to keep treatment objectives consonant with the basic overall objectives of the institution.

Chapter 4

DIFFERENT SETTINGS

Counseling takes place in a wide variety of situations, ranging from those that look very much like outpatient clinics to locked and barred cells in a maximum security institution. Physical surroundings are probably less important than many other aspects of the counseling process or program. But ease of accessibility to sessions may be fairly important to the continuity of a group or program as well as the content of the discussions. The following section traces an individual through the criminal justice process, highlighting the kinds of counseling that he or she might encounter at the various stages.

PROBATION[1]

Because individuals on probation have relative freedom of movement, they receive a high proportion of correctional counseling. Probationers are viewed as needing considerable guidance in terms of simple, factual information that enables them to work with welfare agencies, relate to the court system, deal with landlords, and secure and maintain employment. Probation officers frequently find themselves forced into the role of family counselor with both youthful offenders who reside at home and individuals who are married. While some probation supervisors believe that family therapy or counseling should be undertaken only by pro-

---

[1]This refers to a sentence served under supervision in the community in lieu of incarceration.

fessionals in this field, most feel that the probation officer can contribute positively in all areas of life adjustment.

In recent years group counseling has come to assume a more significant role in probation supervision. Especially with juveniles, the tendency to gather in clubs or gangs seems to make them natural candidates for group counseling. Group counseling has been found to be very helpful in adult probation, too. For one thing, almost all probation caseloads are larger than the supervisors feel are appropriate. Group counseling offers the only opportunity for many officers to maintain contact with those for whom they have responsibility.

For example, Faust (1965) reported on the use of nongroup-trained probation officers in handling group supervision. With a fairly sizeable sample (N=24) it was found that while there was no difference in the number of probationers committing new offenses, a much higher percentage completed their probation with a rating of satisfactory adjustment than did a control group under normal supervision (43% vs. 30% for the comparison group). Of even greater importance is the fact that this procedure nearly doubled contact between officer and client.

At about the same time Mandel (1965) reported on a different approach to the measurement of recidivism. He noted that those under group supervision (15-man group meetings for 90 minutes every two weeks) had a lower rate of revocation. They also demonstrated a higher ratio of months without revocation to months at risks than did a control group. Also, the group approach was less costly than individual supervision.

In California, the *"probation subsidy"* program (Saleeby, 1971) gave additional impetus to such efforts. This program was developed as an outgrowth of early community-based enthusiasm. A detailed review of the records of individuals sent to state-level correctional facilities revealed that from one-fourth to one-third of those individuals being admitted could have been handled safely under probationary supervision had local jurisdictions been able to provide suitable programs (Smith, 1965; Roberts & Sekel, 1965). Plans then evolved to reimburse counties for each individual they did *not* previously send to a state facility. The money, however, could not be used to support existing services but had to be spent on carefully planned, improved services. Of the "improved services," many involved counseling and considerable group interaction of one kind or another.

JAIL

Suppose that the individual is not given probation but rather is sentenced to a local jail? What are his chances of getting some help through counseling? The answer is, "rather slim." In a few of the larger jail programs across the country, some counseling is available and programs have been initiated (Fenton, 1961). However, they consistently lack continuity of effort, and very little counseling actually takes place in the jail setting. This phenomenon is particularly devastating when one realizes that the vast majority of offenders are incarcerated at the local level.

Including juvenile halls under the heading of local incarceration brightens the picture somewhat, for communities are generally concerned about the juvenile offender and quite often attempt to provide some sort of counseling activity. Again, however, continuity of application is probably not great.

Recently the Federal Bureau of Prisons initiated a massive building program for Metropolitan Community Centers to house federal offenders in humane jail settings. These centers opened in 1974 and 1975 in San Diego, Chicago, and New York City. They provide a modern highrise facility with staffing patterns conducive to counseling.

Other similar facilities are being planned and should help greatly to solve the problems of overcrowded jails and the lack of humane rehabilitative programs.

Prison

It is within major correctional institutions, particularly the prison, that the greatest application of counseling is found. In prison, counseling efforts range from individual career guidance and emotional counseling, to small group counseling and family therapy, to large group interaction and therapeutic community programs. However, the bulk of counseling in the prison setting has been some kind of small group interaction. The group counseling model developed by Norman Fenton (1950) rapidly spread throughout the nation. Small groups with a strong Transactional Analytic orientation are also increasing. The added dimension of Carkhuff's helping techniques (Carkhuff, 1968) are being applied with both individuals and groups.

Guided group interaction programs and "therapeutic communities" now dot the correctional landscape, and model institutional designs are sometimes planned around the therapeutic community concept (Bradley, 1969; Saleeby, 1970).

The In-Between Stage—Halfway Houses

With the current emphasis upon community-based corrections, a variety of way-stations have been created including community correctional centers, group homes, halfway houses, work furlough units, and community program centers. Group counseling and therapeutic communities thrive in these settings where they are probably necessary. Counselees are subject to the stress of being neither an inmate nor a parolee, but suffering the disadvantages of each status. This leads to a variety of problems that some sort of group interaction can ameliorate. In addition, there are stresses associated with the transitional process from being closely controlled to being moderately responsible for a large portion of one's life. Again, insights developed in the security of the institutional setting can be tested out in the arena of life in a semi-protected community.

Any group of people attempting to conduct their lives in close juxtaposition will require some mechanism for conflict resolution. Thus, we see that halfway houses and correctional centers tend to incorporate not only group counseling and therapeutic community concepts but also self-help efforts toward personal skill development. Some self-help programs go well beyond the use of the group as an adjunct to regular programs and make it a central focus of their intervention strategies. Synanon might be an example of this.

PAROLE[2]

The major portion of the parole agent's time is spent on individual counseling. Although some of it is quite directive, a great deal of it is devoted to sympathetic attempts to help the individual understand the adjustment process.

In recent years group counseling has emerged in parole, much as it has in probation, to help the agent increase communication with his clients, and to improve their interpersonal skills.

Group counseling in the parole setting provides continuity in counseling from the institutional system to the freer society of the community. In the institutional setting the individual can only talk about what he *might* do in a

[2]This term refers to a period of supervision following incarceration.

given situation. Counseling under parole supervision deals with what he actually *did* in reaction to certain stressful situations or what he is *doing* in response to the stresses of new problems.

SUMMARY

Counselors in corrections may find themselves taking such widely varied approaches as visiting former inmates in their homes to working within the prison atmosphere. As tasks, objectives, and techniques differ, the counselor may be required to assume a number of roles including personal family counselor and/or designer of therapeutic community programs. Group counseling is developing rapidly as an efficient and effective way of providing counseling services in most correctional settings.

Chapter 5

THE DIFFERING LEVELS

The tax structure in government aptly illustrates the complexity of its organization. Each level demands some sort of rebate, subsidy, or revenue-sharing, including the criminal justice system, and particularly the correctional field. As noted previously, most of the offenders who are incarcerated are held in local jurisdictions where revenues are limited and demands are great. Generally speaking, where facilities are most required, incarcerational accomodations are the least adequate. Deficiencies in money for building as well as a scarcity of funds for rehabilitative programs exist. In this chapter several factors that have influenced the direction of counseling efforts at various governmental levels will be briefly explored.

LOCAL EFFORTS

The general inadequacies of counseling activities in jail settings, usually controlled by local jurisdictions, have been noted. Slightly more activity can be observed in juvenile halls, and probation often makes proportionately greater use of counseling, starting, of course, with direct advice-giving.

Counseling efforts are also rapidly expanding in delinquency prevention programs. How to prevent crime has been a topic of extensive discussion and some action since the turn of the century. The value of such efforts is always debatable because the problem is so difficult to evaluate. Caustic critics contend that all such efforts must have been totally ineffectual considering the present level of crime. Supporters of delinquency prevention efforts think that crime would be even greater without these efforts. It seems likely that programs aimed at preventing delinquency are useful and certainly necessary to an enlightened society that wants to do something to stem the tide of criminal activity. The work of LaMar Empy (1967) serves as an outstanding example of the application of group procedures in this area and will be discussed in greater detail as some of the new, emerging techniques and programs are examined.

State Programs

Much counseling activity takes place at the state level with group counseling as the most common approach. When counseling was in its heyday in California, one institution (California Correctional Institute in Tehachapi), with the cooperation of the inmates developed a group counseling program with 100% participation in lieu of constructing additional fences, gun towers and taking other costly security measures.

Generally speaking, more traditional counseling approaches have been used with the more stabilized inmates. It is with the youthful offender that such innovative practices are being tested as matching clients with counselors, small group homes, and stratified living units.

The Federal System

The correctional apparatus of the federal system parallels that of the states in that the federal system also operates institutional and parole services as well as community program centers (halfway houses) and jail facilities.

In the past, the federal system took a "middle of the

road" stance, tending to provide rather well-established treatment opportunities along orthodox lines. For example, the availability of psychotherapy and specialized counseling was limited to a small number of inmates.

Since the recent initiation of the Omnibus Crime Bill of 1968, however, the federal system has been designated as a model for sound correctional practices. The bill encouraged the already growing awareness of a need for change, with the result that the federal system presently probably does play a leadership role in many areas, especially counseling. In fact, many innovative programs have had their beginnings in federal facilities. At the moment there is experimentation not only with traditional group counseling, but also with peer counseling, token economies, programs relating typology to counseling[1], biofeedback techniques, and innovative drug abuse programs.

SUMMARY

Unfortunately, local jail settings, where most offenders are incarcerated, have the least adequate provisions for rehabilitative efforts. However preventive programs at the local level are receiving more attention. States are attempting to develop counseling programs, especially in group format, and especially with youthful offenders. Recent legislation has encouraged federal institutions to provide leadership in counseling programs and to experiment with innovative approaches that may become models for other institutions in designing their own efforts.

---

[1]The Quay (1964) typology has been widely used in federal youth and juvenile facilities, and has met with relative success in relating typology to program efforts.

Chapter 6

NEW APPROACHES

Some of the approaches outlined in this chapter have been alluded to earlier. In general, most of the techniques that will be discussed can be seen in only one or two settings; a few have started to permeate the field. Traditionally, treatment has used techniques that were initially employed in mental health settings or educational facilities. The viability of this procedure has sometimes been questionable, but, by and large, most such techniques have been fairly well adopted and have become rather standardized practice. However, several new approaches have been conceived and developed within the correctional framework.

GROUP HOMES

Institutionalizing the juvenile delinquent, the predelinquent, and those in-need-of-care has always been viewed as negative. Since foster homes are considered preferable, efforts have been made to provide such care for many of these young people. Needless to say, the sheer volume precludes finding enough homes. And even when homes are found, the social climate may not be beneficial for the client.

As noted previously, juveniles have a tendency to flock together and form clubs, organizations, or gangs. It seems entirely logical that some effort be made to provide living arrangements that will capitalize on this. At the same time, a small group of parent surrogates can be trained for the more economical placement of larger numbers of young delinquents and predelinquents. Within this framework, considerable work has been done to match both counselor and setting with *groups* of individuals with similar personality or adjustment problems. While preliminary evidence suggests that this may be an efficient and effective approach, in no way is it a panacea.

MATCHING CLIENT AND COUNSELOR

One of the best attempts to match client and counselor is by the application of theoretical typology, which involves levels of interpersonal maturity (I-level). Developed in a naval disciplinary barracks (Sullivan, Grant and Grant, 1957), this theory proposes that youthful offenders can be classified according to their view of significant others, particularly authority figures, in their immediate social/psychological environment. Classification levels range from I-1 to I-7, that is, from the least mature to the most mature. Examination of the clientele in correctional settings suggests that most offenders can be classified between I-2 and I-4 or I-5.

The less mature tend to view authority figures as givers or withholders of the good things in life and often try to obtain what they want through a straight demand system. As their interpersonal maturity increases, they begin to see that the quality of others' response to them largely depends upon their good behavior. Some will then embark upon a pattern of extreme conformity, continually seeking love and praise from parental figures and others in authority. Others at this level learn the motivations behind other people's actions and consequently learn how to shape these motivations for their own ends. The ultimate abuser of this approach is the very smooth "con-man" manipulator.

As the individual's personal maturity increases, he or she internalizes standards of conduct to judge himself or herself against. However, this may result in anxiety and tension when behavior falls short of goals and expectations. In the most mature individuals, altruistic motivations become a part of the total personality structure.

In what probably represents one of the better studies in interactional psychotherapy, the Camp Elliot study (Grant and Grant, 1959) matched groups of individuals classified in terms of this theory with different kinds of group leaders. The findings suggest that those with lower levels of maturity respond *less* well to counseling and/or therapeutic approaches than do those at more mature levels. On the other hand, the group made up of people with lower levels of maturity tended to respond quite well to highly authoritarian group leaders who might be characterized as DI's (Marine drill instructors). The group made up of I-4's and I-5's did not respond as positively to the authoritarian approach, nor as negatively to counseling kinds of interventions.

Starting from a rather simple, skeletal system of typologies, the classification scheme now has become far more elaborate and includes more subtle classifications for various subtypes. A wide variety of intervention strategies have also been identified for each of the different levels and subtypes. The Community Treatment Project (Warren, 1965), which developed specialized group homes, applied the theory extensively.

A number of typology systems has been developed, some for diagnostic purposes only and others for classification for treatment. The Quay-Peterson (1958) represents one of the latter efforts. That particular classification system as modified by Quay and Parsons (1971) played an integral role in the special treatment program combining token economy with counseling developed for Morgantown (also used now in Oxford, Wisconsin, FCI). It represents a systematic development different from fairly classical psychiatric diagnostic categories.

Use of Testing in Counseling

After almost any kind of typology is developed, the next step is to test the efficiency of the classification by evaluation. In the case of the Quay-Peterson, the test preceded program uses of the diagnostic categories. In the I-level approach, initial classification was dependent upon a long, involved, and quite complicated individual diagnostic interview. Subsequently, more objective, easily administered psychometric devices were developed to provide a fairly reliable indication of interpersonal maturity levels.

Other settings and jurisdictions have attempted to match client and counselor through some sort of testing program, but no major systematic approach has evolved. For example, the Federal Prison System uses the Minnesota Multiphasic Personality Inventory throughout the system, but with limited application. One exception is the work of Magargee and his associates at The Florida State University in cooperation with the Tallahassee Federal Institution. This effort has produced a series of FCI Reports leading to such novel concepts as "over-controlled hostility," and has the aim of classifying inmates according to treatment goals.[1]

While diagnostic testing and psychological evaluations have always been aimed at helping the counselor to better understand the client, seldom has such knowledge been used systematically. Within the last few years, however, growing use has been made of the FIRO-B (Schultz, 1967), Fundamental Interpersonal Relationship Orientation-Behavior. Within several areas this quick paper and pencil test assesses the kind of responses an individual would like to receive when participating in interpersonal interactions. At the same time, it reveals the willingness of the individual

---

[1]Copies of these FCI Reports may be obtained by requests through the Tallahassee, FCI, Psychological Services Department.

to *give* to such interactions. In an ideal situation, for example, a counselor with strong nurturing needs can be paired up with a client who strongly needs to be nurtured in his interpersonal interactions. In the usual case, the counselor may not feel totally comfortable in providing assistance to meet the particular needs of the client, but can at least identify what kind of response might prove helpful and attempt to work within that framework.

Although testing has always been prevalent throughout the justice system, much of it has been done by academic researchers, mainly interested in studying the inhabitants of a microcosm of society. In effect, this approach treats prisons and their inmates as guinea pigs. Because the caged have become test-weary, meaningful functional research has become more difficult to carry out. To help solve the problem, the Federal Bureau of Prisons is beginning to establish research positions within institutions. The new Federal Facility at Butner, North Carolina, will be designed to include a volunteer research center providing more information on how to treat chronic offenders. A more enlightened use of testing in counseling and classification should come about with the help of highly trained professionals and paraprofessional staff and executive leadership by educationally and psychologically oriented individuals. Hopefully this approach would serve as a national model for other facilities.

GIMMICKS AND GADGETRY

Tape recording has long been an invaluable aid in training counselors and has also been used to help a group get a better understanding of their own patterns of interaction. Of even greater impact is the use of video tape feedback where the individual can actually *see* how he is coming across to others.

Biofeedback techniques, especially galvanic skin responses, have been utilized to help both counselor and counselee more clearly determine when areas of high emotional content are being tapped. While biofeedback techniques are in the early experimental stages, they are being used in Lompoc, California, FCI and being developed at Milan FCI as part of a drug abuse program.

Peer Counseling

Since the late 40's offenders have been used irregularly to carry on counseling activities, a practice known as peer counseling. Studies have clearly demonstrated that prisoners can be trained to handle groups as effectively as most people. Probably the most well known and well developed program in peer counseling is that operating out of two federal institutions and one prison in California. This program has a structured system for group training and a graduated approach for developing group counselors or leaders. Preliminary phases begin with heavy doses of didactic lectures in Transactional Analysis supplemented by a practicum. After rather extensive training, the client is then ready to function as an assistant instructor or as a coleader in small group counseling. Advanced stages of the peer counseling program include learning the elements of group interaction, leadership dynamics, the organization of treatment efforts, and Carkhuff's (1968) helping techniques. Preliminary evaluations have been consistently positive. One particular result is that prisoners who act as counseling leaders seldom become involved in disciplinary difficulty. Followup studies of former prisoner/counselors indicate a carry-over of improvement from the prison to society-at-large.

Peer counseling as a form of group counseling is fairly economical. Also, because material aid is offered to those who undergo the training, the program functions as a whole life style reorientation system. In view of the benefits, minimal cost, and the self-help orientation, it seems likely that this is an approach that will soon spread across the nation.

The Offender as Consultant/Counselor

Utilizing the offender as consultant/counselor is not counseling in the usual sense, but is being so considered because the interactions and goals parallel those of counseling.

College programs in sociology and criminology geared toward a realistic understanding of justice and correctional problems frequently invite former prisoners to provide a view of correctional institutions from a slightly different perspective. This practice has grown to the point where individuals particularly skilled in talking to groups are employed as consultants to educational institutions or programs and occasionly become staff instructors. In addition many such individuals are employed by special interest reform groups to assist with lobbying in legislatures. As in the case of peer counseling, the participant tends to realign his values as he works more closely with the "establishment."

The specialized training of clients to function as counselors in specialized areas is similar. For example, former narcotic offenders are considered to be particularly gifted as counselors to predelinquents to help prevent the abuse of drugs, including alcohol.

While a number of programs have been instituted along this line, SPAN is the one most familiar to the authors. Nissen (1970) set up a program wherein potential counselors are selected from an inmate population during the later phases of their incarceration. While in the correctional institution they start college work and training and upon release continue with an intensive training program for paraprofessionals on a regular college campus. While this program has not been without trials, completely trained would-be counselors have been placed in school districts to assist in drug abuse prevention programs.

SUMMARY

New approaches for correctional counseling include group homes, matching client and counselor, the use of testing and audio-visual technology, peer counseling, and training the offender for consulting or counseling. Although each of these approaches require more evaluation, preliminary studies indicate they are having at least some success.

Chapter 7

STUDIES OF EFFECTIVENESS

> Although counseling is not always effective in reducing parole violations or recidivism, it is usually effective in reducing misbehavior within the institutions. Counseling juveniles seems to yield better results than counseling adults.

That counseling has not been as carefully evaluated as many other correctional practices is the keynote of the summary of research on group methods in Lipton, Martinson, and Wilkes (1975):

> Considering the amount of support group treatment methods have received, it is surprising that there are so few reliable and valid findings concerning their effectiveness. In addition, where favorable results are found, reductions in recidivism were relatively small. (p. 278)

The survey of research indicates that, while counseling has not made any major impact on reducing recidivism, it is effective in ameliorating institutional difficulties. A number of studies are reviewed suggesting that matching clients with counseling approaches can be a significant factor in the program's success. In reviewing the significant studies in the field, emphasis will be on those illustrating positive application.

Kassebaum, Ward and Wilner

This unique study is probably one of the best controlled studies to test the effectiveness of various counseling approaches (1971). The setting for the study was California Men's Colony at San Luis Obispo. At the time of the study it was a new medium security institution in the California Department of Corrections divided into four quads with central services, a near ideal design for accommodating different kinds of programs.

In the four quads the following types of counseling were established:

1. Voluntary group counseling. (As a natural result, a subgroup of *voluntary non-participation* was also created.)
2. Mandatory intensive counseling by specially trained counselors.
3. Large-group community living. This included small-group counseling along with frequent large-group meetings.
4. Regular institutional program with no group counseling available.

The subjects were nearly 1000 young adult male offenders, 18 years of age or older, with the majority of the group between the ages of 20 to 27. For 6 months to 2 years individuals participated in the treatment and were followed up after institutional release for a period of 36 months.

From official publications, and with the help of institutional personnel, an attempt was made to identify the objectives of the program. Two major points evolved:

1. Group counseling should reduce involvement in institutional disciplinary infractions.

2. Counseling should facilitate adjustment following release, leading to an improved parole outcome.

Group 4 served as a control group. No differences were observed between any of the treatment groups and the control group in the proportions of individuals who were able to remain discipline-free during their institutional stay. About half of each group managed this level of adjustment. There were no significant differences among the groups in regard to the types of rule infractions.

Concerning recidivism, after 36 months there were no significant differences between the groups. Significantly, there was no difference in the outcome for those who were counseled by the regular lay staff with normal departmental group counseling instructions and those who were counseled by highly specialized counselors.

THE HIGHFIELDS PROGRAM

The Highfields Program is one of the earliest and most successful efforts at milieu therapy. It involved large group interaction with small guided group programs that dealt with informal inmate-staff interaction. Freeman and Weeks (1956) report on 237 male offenders in the 16–18 age group who went through the program for 6 months. They found that those going through the Highfields Program had more success with staying out of trouble than those released from a regular institution at a significant ratio of 63% versus 43%. Inasmuch as operation costs of the two programs were similar, it was felt that the project was not only effective in reducing recidivism, but it also had a favorable cost/benefit ratio.

Joplin (1968, 1971) reports additional information about this program as well as others involving group interaction.

Table 7.1 Studies of Psychiatric Evaluations of Offenders

Source	Population	Diagnosis	Percent
Glueck (1918)	608 Sing Sing prisoners	Psychotic or mentally deteriorated	12.0
		Normal	41.0
		Mentally retarded	28.1
Overholser (1935)	5,000 felons under Briggs Law in Massachusetts	Abnormal	15.0
		Normal	85.0
Bromberg and Thompson (1937)	9,958 offenders before Court of General Sessions, New York City	Psychotic	1.5
		Psychoneurotic	6.9
		Psychopathic personalities	6.9
		Feebleminded	2.4
		Normal or mild personality defects	82.3
Schilder (1940)	Convicted felons, Court of General Sessions of New York City	Psychotic	1.6
		Neurotic	4.2
		Psychopathic personalities	7.3
		Feebleminded	3.1
		Normal	83.8
Banay (1941)	Sing Sing prisoners	Psychotic	1.0
		Emotionally immature	20.0
		Psychopathic	17.0
		Normal	62.0
Poindexter (1955)	100 problem inmates	Mentally ill	20.0
		Normal	80.0
Schlessinger and Blau (1957)	500 typical prisoners	Character and behavior disorders	85.0
		Normal	15.0
Shands (1958)	1,720 North Carolina felon admissions to Central Prison	Psychotic	3.5
		Personality disorder	55.8
		Psychoneurotic	3.9
		Sociopathic personality	7.0
		Other	5.3
		No psychiatric disorder	4.7
		Transient personality disorder	19.8
Brodsky (1970)	32,511 military prisoners	Character and behavior disorders	77.1
		No psychiatric disease	21.3
		Miscellaneous disease	1.6

LAMAR EMPEY

Lamar Empey has given considerable impetus to the community-based correctional effort. The bulk of his work has been setting up programs for juveniles and youthful offenders that aim to prevent incarceration. His first project, the Provo experiment, involved daily group sessions in a milieu therapy atmosphere. The program involved 200 juvenile offenders between the ages of 15 and 17 who underwent treatment for approximately 7 months. After 6 months, little difference was reported between the outcome of those assigned to the experimental program and those assigned to regular probation. However, a much higher percentage of those *completing* the experimental program were arrest-free during the followup period than of those completing regular probation. Those going through either experimental program or regular probation did significantly better than those who had been assigned to the reformatory (Empey, 1966).

In a later program in California, a community-based semi-institutional setting again used milieu therapy and guided group interaction. This program was compared with a small institution that placed emphasis on skill development and maturation. A 1-year followup study was conducted, involving 84 boys, ages 16 to 18. Half of those completing the experimental program were involved in further offenses compared with 75% of those from the institution.

THE YOUTH CENTER RESEARCH PROJECT

The Youth Center Research Project was a large-scale project carried out in the Stockton complex of the California Youth Authority. Following one of the most rigorous designs for studying the effectiveness of different kinds of treatment interventions, it studied Transactional Analysis and behavior modification.

One major hypothesis of the project was that Transactional Analysis would be more effective with higher maturity level youthful male offenders, and behavior modification with less verbal, lower maturity level subjects. Another major hypothesis was that both treatment intervention strategies would be more effective than a regular institutional program involving group and individual counseling.

Two small institutions of comparable size and staffing were each given an individual mission. One was 100% oriented toward Transactional Analysis while the other was totally committed to behavior modification, involving a token economy. The staff members of the two institutions received extensive and intensive training in the treatment modality with which they were to become involved. A group of 1,130 offenders between the ages of 16 and 20 were randomly assigned to the two facilities. Of those assigned 160 had completed the program at one institution and 144 had completed at the time of the preliminary followup.

Results of the program include the following:

1. Although initially the number of incidents and misconduct reports rose markedly, the number of incidents and the amount of time spent in detention was later reduced by more than 60% in both units.
2. In both programs, the more mature residents responded more favorably, a finding that probably should have been expected.
3. In terms of psychological outlook, Transactional Analysis participants changed more than those in behavior modification in the following ways:
    A. Reduced feelings of anxiety and depression
    B. More positive self-concept

C. More optimistic about the future
D. More determination and confidence in their ability

4. Participants in the Transactional Analysis program were more positive in their evaluation of the school's activities and more accepting of staff. Behavior ratings, however, showed that those undergoing behavior modification improved slightly more than those who had participated in the TA program.

5. The reports on the first 427 participants who had been released for a period of 12 months after participating in the project showed a 31% rate of failures on parole for one group versus 32% for the other, suggesting no difference between the two treatment approaches. However, both violation rates were significantly lower than the 43% rate of violations for those who had gone through the same institutions prior to the experimental program and considerably lower than the 46% rate of violations for a group of a comparable age released from the other Youth Authority institutions.

Thus, it would appear that either intervention strategy is equally successful and that counseling *can* be effective in reducing recidivism rates if given total institution commitment (Jesness, 1972).

SUMMARY

This quick review reveals that the findings do not strongly support claims for great gains from correctional counseling. On the other hand, there are indications that some kinds of treatment intervention do make a difference, and often a significant one. As we look at those areas where there is a finding of "no difference," such as the Kassebaum, Ward and Wilner study, we see a retreat to an older attitude viewing all inmates, their needs, and motivations as identical. We all know that inmates are not peas in a pod, yet time and time again we institute programs in a blanket fashion thinking that perhaps they will be successful in dealing with at least *some* clients. They seldom are.

It seems that developments in the field should now be sophisticated enough to deal with this kind of problem more effectively. The Camp Elliot study (Grant and Grant, 1959) indicates that different kinds of people respond differently to different kinds of leadership. The PICO project (Adams, 1961) shows that applying treatment intervention to those for whom it is inappropriate may be more harmful than helpful. In that study, those classified as "unamenable" *and who were given individual and group counseling* did considerably less well on parole than did those who received no counseling at all, whether they were classified as amenable or not amenable. More recently the Community Treatment Program (Warren, 1965) delineates the interaction between different kinds of supervision and different kinds of clients to show the relationship of interaction to positive parole adjustment. Thus, as one looks to the future, it is hoped that more attention will be paid to characteristics of clients and the kinds of approaches or techniques most likely to result in a beneficial outcome.

Chapter 8

SOME PRACTICAL GUIDES TOWARD APPLICATION

Although several waves of enthusiasm over group counseling and therapeutic communities have swept over the nation's prisons, there may be some institutions or newly initiated programs that have not yet tried these approaches. The following suggestions are set forth for the guidance of those who are planning counseling programs, with the hope that they will be of practical value.

EXAMINE THE CLIENTELE

Too often in the correctional process we develop an ideal program and then look around to see if we can find inmates or probationers to fit into it. A better approach is to first examine the needs of the individuals, and then determine what kinds of programs might meet these needs. This can be done by using one of the established classification systems employing typologies, or by developing and initiating one's own battery of instruments to obtain a better knowledge of the clientele. Any typology used must be evaluated against the particular situation in which the counseling program is to be implemented. For example, the I-level approach might be best for one program, while some sort of behavioral index might be more appropriate for another.

Some would say that categorizing is often more harmful than useful. Once someone has been tested, categorized, and labeled, further understanding of that person is often impaired, and the label becomes a self-fulfilling prophecy of that person's behavior patterns. Also, when one is labeled certain attributes become attached to that person that may not exist. Avoiding the use of typologies could minimize the negative offshoots of labeling.

OUTLINE YOUR OBJECTIVES

Counseling objectives can be outlined in a number of ways. Arnold (1974) discusses such items as:

> "to prepare inmates for socially accepted lives in the community with subobjectives being: (1) the creation of subcultures that will support conforming behavior and condemn illegal behavior, (2) development of peer pressure for conforming behavior, and (3) adoption of realistic and appropriate perceptions of values and expected behavior."

Such objectives would be very difficult to measure. One would have to assume certain logical consequences deriving from attainment of these objectives, thus generating indirect hypotheses. For example, the primary objective of "socially acceptable lives in the community" might be translated to mean "arrest-free for a specified period." Certainly, this objective is easier to measure than one more broadly stated. However, sometimes it may be advantageous to set up objectives in terms of broadly stated goals.

One such objective might be the "enhancement of feelings of involvement on the part of the staff." Although it is broadly stated and subjective, this objective may not be unnecessarily difficult to measure. In surveying attitudes of California Correctional personnel, for example, Kassebaum, Ward and Wilner (1963) found that:

> Participation in counseling may alleviate feelings of being left out of the important work of the prison. The data indicate that those involved in the treatment program have an

outlook more in line with the philosophy behind the program than do staff members who are not counselors.

Other possible objectives are:

1. Improving institutional climate. This objective has not been dealt with extensively in the literature of research; however, with the development of institution climate scales, it is now possible to document changes.
2. Lowering the rate of disciplinary difficulties. Simple bookkeeping should reveal whether this objective has been achieved. Research in this area has already shown positive results, and easy ways are available for assessing goal achievement (Griedland, 1960; Truax, 1966).
3. Reducing recidivism. Although this can be difficult to measure, it is an important criterion for evaluating a correctional program. It is important, therefore, that this objective be stated clearly, and the methodology be developed to insure its accurate measurement.
4. Positive shifts in personality. Standardized personality tests could be used to measure the achievement of this objective.

Establishing measurable objectives gives the program a basis for evaluation. Whether or not a program has been successful—and even its *degree* of success—can be determined by measuring the extent to which objectives have been met. Furthermore, making established measurable objectives known to both counselors and clients can give direction and purpose to counseling programs, which, in itself, facilitates progress.

SURVEY COUNSELING APPROACHES

It is usually recognized that the counseling approach used in any program should be compatible with the needs, clientele, and objectives of that program. Other factors to be considered include the cost of implementing a particular approach, the relevant resources available to the institution, and the expertise and attitudes of the staff members who will be conducting the program.

Program Costs

The cost of a program is affected by the number of staff required (and their level of training), by necessary special materials or resources, and by the number of staff hours required for program implementation.

Outside consultants usually bolster a program. When consultants are used, it is wise and economical to select a program for which expert assistance is available locally.

A program may require special materials ranging from books and other printed matter for distributing occupational information to specially designed buildings or building wings for therapeutic communities. Many counseling methods need little more than a room in which to meet, whereas others, like biofeedback, require special equipment. The cost of buying, renting, or leasing needed materials and resources should be assessed.

The number of staff hours needed to implement a program refers to the ratio between staff hours spent and number of persons counseled. Comparing group counseling with individual counseling best illustrates the impact that this has on a program. However, this is not the only factor. For any program to be effective, staff time will be spent on noncounseling functions, such as making special preparations, and this, too, should be assessed.

Available Resources

The cost incurred by special materials or resources for a counseling program can be reduced if some of those resources are already available to the institution. Even if available resources are not essential to program implementation, they may still be helpful in achieving program objectives.

Human resources should be considered as well as material ones. For example, if occupational training is a component of your program, local tradesmen and/or businessmen could be invited in to demonstrate and teach their skills.

Expertise and Attitudes of Staff

The impact of staff expertise on program costs has already been touched on, but the assessment of this impact could be more complicated than was implied. While highly trained professionals earn higher salaries than minimally trained or paraprofessional staff, they may also be more efficient. Some studies have shown that counseling by peers or paraprofessionals can be just as effective as counseling by an experienced professional—but only for certain types of counseling and certain objectives.

The attitudes of the staff are also important for program success. An unpopular program may fail simply because of the lack of enthusiasm and commitment that are required for success.

Assessing Alternative Programs

In order to adequately assess the compatibility of a program to institutional needs and objectives and determine its probable cost and effectiveness, more than a review of the literature is needed. The best sources of information are other institutions that have a program similar to the one you are considering. Information from these sources can be obtained via letters, telephone conversations, or site visits, depending on budget allowances.

Staff Selection

It is vital that care be taken in selecting any additional staff, especially those who will be program leaders. Arnold (1974) cites two especially important characteristics: skill in communication techniques and a personal warmth with good ego strength.

Selection can be effectively carried out if three fairly simple criteria are applied: (1) candidates must be highly motivated and interested; (2) they should be humanistically oriented; and (3) they must be flexible enough to benefit from a training program which may lead them to alter preconceived views.

Staff Training

Orientation sessions for the staff should start well in advance of program implementation beginning with top staff, who can later assist with orienting the rest of the staff.

It is advisable to design specific training modules with clearly defined objectives. The modules insure that the trainees know how far they have progressed, while the objectives allow them to know when they have arrived at the desired level of competency. Training objectives should be clearly stated. It should constantly be made clear to participants that they are not expected to perform some task for which they are unprepared, and that they will be placed in a given activity only when they are fully trained for that activity. If trainees know exactly what is expected of them, their anxieties can be allayed to a great extent.

Organizational Structure

If a program is to be successful, the supervisor should report directly to the highest administrator in the program's system. Otherwise programs become subordinate to the ongoing traditional activities and are seldom effective. Although several questions of priority must be determined early, the crucial question is whether counseling or other types of training or education will take precedence.

The setting for treatment is also highly important. Ideally, the total institution should be dedicated to the program to be initiated. Chamlee (1967) clearly defines some of the problems that can be encountered when attempting to integrate a program into ongoing institutional operations. Such attempts are viewed as "elitist," and "sibling rivalries" develop as other segments of the program view the special treatment section as receiving preferential consideration. This conflict often leads to a subtle sabotaging of the program and verbal undermining of program objectives. A program in this kind of setting will have difficulty initiating procedures that are not congruent with traditional activities.

This problem may be overcome, however, by somehow involving those individuals with the strongest opposition to or resentment of the program. In fulfilling their new duties, they may become strong program supporters.

Another difficulty in integrating a program within a larger institutional or program setting is known as "radiation of effects." Competition and exchange of ideas leads to a spread of the positive aspects of the program to comparison or control situations. This impairs evaluation efforts by minimizing differences between the experimental and control groups.

A well-articulated organizational structure is necessary to support the program. This includes ongoing training programs to keep counselors who have undergone initial training up-to-date in their skills. In addition, new counselors must be constantly trained for replacements as transfers and promotions occur, and to activate new groups within an expanding program.

Organizational support is also necessary to develop a

monitoring system for ongoing counseling activity. Such monitoring insures the quality of counseling and maintains consistency with whatever theoretical approach is chosen. Without such constraints, programs tend to become quite amorphous and ill-defined. Activities within the group take on the character of the personality of the leader and may range from didactic lectures, to amateur religious services, to exercises in the formation of democratic structures. It is doubtful that all such approaches, however valuable, fit in a single, predetermined treatment approach. Inconsistent counseling renders evaluations of little consequence, for those interpreting the results would be uncertain as to what activities the observed results are attributable.

An Overview

This monograph presented a short history of correctional counseling followed by an examination of correct counseling approaches. This was accompanied by an explanation of how the setting, clientele, and level of corrections should be considered to determine the counseling method to be used. A corollary of this last factor is considering the individual needs of clients, and how they lend themselves to various counseling methods. New, innovative approaches to correctional counseling were particularly spotlighted. These approaches included matching client and counselor, peer counseling programs, group homes for juveniles, and therapeutic communities.

A few studies of the effectiveness of correctional counseling were also reviewed. Results tend to show that, while counseling has not yet been as effective as we would like, the outcome is usually an improvement of institutional climate and, in a few cases, of parole adjustment.

This review was followed by some guidelines for implementing counseling programs in correctional institutions. Emphasis was placed upon the importance of clearly defined objectives and the importance of matching the counseling program with the institution's objectives and resources. The process of staff selection and staff training was also discussed.

Now is the time to move forward with careful applications of the various counseling techniques. Particular care must be taken to evaluate efforts to determine if and where gains are being made. After carefully appraising our efforts, we must align them with realistic goals. While counselors and therapists have often felt they have the answers to recidivism and other crime, these problems are linked to sociological and economic variables, and cannot be solved by counseling alone. We can, though, provide humanistic environments wherein offenders can learn alternative approaches to their problems. Counseling is an important part of this effort.

The age of "treatment," with its connotations of "illness," and the forced application of "cures" is ending, with the emergence of a more enlightened approach. This approach involves integrated programs designed to facilitate the learning of those social skills necessary to freely choose a life style that is rewarding for both the individual and society. All involved are models and teachers, and the offenders are treated with fairness and respect, thereby reducing anger and emotionality and enhancing the learning process.

We cannot continue to coerce offenders into conformity. We must provide those experiences necessary to individual adjustment and a meaningful life. For most people this comes through opportunities for intellectual and emotional growth. Why not for offenders?

REFERENCES

Adams, S. Interaction between individual interview therapy and treatment amenability in older Youth Authority wards. In *Inquiries concerning kinds of treatment for kinds of delinquents* (Monograph No. 29). Sacramento, Calif.: California Board of Corrections, 1961. (Republished by N. Johnston, *The sociology of punishment and correction.* New York: John Wiley & Sons, 1962).

Arnold, W. R. Group methods in correctional treatment. In R. R. Roberts (Ed.), *Correctional treatments of the offender.* Springfield, Ill.: Charles C Thomas, 1974, 176–194.

Arnold, W. R., & Stiles, B. A summary of increasing use of "group methods" in corrections. *International Journal of Group Therapy,* 1972, *22,* 78–93. (Summary)

Bandura, A. *Principles of behavior modification.* New York: Holt, Rinehart & Winston, 1969.

Barry, J. V. Pioneers in criminology XII: Alexander Maconochie (1787–1860). *Journal of Criminal Law, Criminology and Police Science,* 1965, *47,* 145–161.

Berne, E. *Transactional analysis in psychotherapy.* New York: Grove Press, 1961.

Bradley, H. B., Smith, G. B., & Salstrom, W. H. *A design for change.* Sacramento, Calif.: American Justice Institute, 1969.

Brodsky, S. L. *Psychologists in the criminal justice system.* Chicago: University of Illinois Press, 1973, 149–155.

Carkhuff, R. R. *Helping and human relations. Vol. I. Selection and training. Vol. II. Practice and research.* New York: Holt, Rinehart & Winston, 1969.

Carhuff, R. R., & Truax, C. B. Lay mental health counseling: The effects of lay group counseling. *Journal of Consulting Psychology,* 1965, *29,* 426–431.

Carter, R. M., Glasser, D., & Wilkins, L. T. *Correctional institutions.* New York: Lippincott, 1972.

Chamlee, F. A. Administrative considerations in the correctional community. In N. Fenton, E. Reimer, & H. Wilner (Eds.) *The correctional community: An introduction and guide.* Berkeley, Calif.: University of California Press, 1967.

Cressey, D. R. Changing criminals: The application of the theory of differential association. *American Journal of Sociology,* 1955, *61,* 116–120.

Dunbar, W. *Should the offender be required to accept treatment?* Presented at the American Orthopsychiatric Association's 43rd Annual Meeting on April 14, 1966 at San Francisco, Calif. as cited by Sandhu.

Efthihiades, T. D., & Fink, L. A study regarding the value of psychotherapy in prison. *Criminoligica,* 1968, *6*(1), 50–56.

Ellis, A. The treatment of a psychopath with rational therapy. *Journal of Psychology,* 1961, *51*(142).

Empey, L. *Alternative to incarceration.* (J. D. Publication No. 9001). Washington, D. C.: U. S. Department of Health, Education and Welfare, 1967.

Ernst, F. The use of transactional analysis in prison therapy groups. *Correctional Psychiatry and Journal of Social Therapy,* 1962, *8,* 120–132.

Faust, F. L. Group counseling with juveniles by staff without professional training in group work. *Crime and Delinquency,* 1965, *11,* 349–354.

Fenton, N. *An introduction to group counseling in state correctional systems.* New York: American Correctional Association, 1958.

Finney, B. C. The peer group: An experiment in humanistic education. In Bloom, E. L., *Psychological stress in the campus community: Theory, research and action.* New York: Behavioral Publications, 1970.

Freeman, H. E., & Weeks, H. A. Analysis of a program of treatment of delinquent boys. *American Journal of Sociology,* 1956, *62,* 56–61.

Friedland, D. M. *Group counseling as a factor in reducing runaway behavior from an open treatment institution for delinquent and pre-delinquent boys.* Unpublished doctoral dissertation, New York University, 1960.

Glasser, W. *Reality therapy: A new approach to psychiatry.* New York: Harper & Row, 1965.

Grant, J. D., & Grant, M. Q. The treatment of nonconformists in the Navy. *Annals of the American Academy of Political Science,* 1959, *322,* 126–135.

Greenspoon, J. *The effect of verbal and non-verbal stimuli on frequency of members of two verbal response classes.* Unpublished doctoral dissertation, Indiana University, 1952.

Groder, M. G. KUID, *Transactional Analysis,* April, 1971, *1*(2), 19.

Harris, T. A. *I'm O.K.—You're O.K.: A practical guide to transactional analysis.* New York: Harper & Row, 1969.

Hosford, R. E. and Moss, C. S. Counseling in prison: Implication for counselor training. In R. E. Hosford and C. S. Moss (Eds.), *The crumbling walls.* Urbana, Ill.: University of Illinois Press, 1975, 91–104.

Hughes, H. Organizing the therapeutic potential of the addict prisoners community. *International Journal of the Addictions,* 1970, *2*(2), 205–223.

Jesness, C. F., De Risi, W. J., McCormick, P. M., & Wedge, R. F. *Youth center project.* Sacramento, Calif.: American Justice Institute, 1972.

Jones, M. *The therapeutic community.* New York: Basic Books, 1953.

REFERENCES

Joplin, G. H. Self-concept and the Highfields program. *Correctional Psychologist*, 1968, *3*, 4–6.

Joplin, G. H. Personal communication, June, 1971.

Kanfer, F. H., & Saslow, G. Behavioral diagnosis. In C. M. Franks (Ed.), *Behavior therapy: Appraisal and status*. New York: McGraw-Hill, 1969, 57–71.

Kassebaum, G. G., Ward, D. A., & Wilner, D. M. *Group treatment by correctional personnel: A survey of California Department of Corrections* (Monograph No. 3). Sacramento, Calif.: Board of Corrections, 1963, 32–33.

Kassebaum, G. G., Ward, D. A., & Wilner, D. M. *Prison treatment and parole survival*. New York: John Wiley & Sons, 1971.

Kirish, B. R. Peer counseling. In R. E. Hosford & C. S. Moss (Eds.), *The crumbling walls: Treatment and counseling of prisoners*. Urbana, Ill.: University of Illinois Press, 1975, 45–52.

Larson, C. *Guided group interaction: Theory and method*. Hennepin County Court Services Department, Minnesota, 1970.

Laws, D. R., & Serber, M. Measurement and evaluation of assertive training with sexual offenders. In R. E. Hosford & C. S. Moss (Eds.), *The crumbling walls: Treatment and counseling of prisoners*. Urbana, Ill.: University of Illinois Press, 1975, 165–174.

Lipton, D., Martinson, R. & Wilkes, J. *The effectiveness of correctional treatment*. New York: Praeger, 1975.

Mandel, N. Recidivism studied and defined. *Journal of Criminal Law, Criminology and Police Science*, 1965, *51*, 59–66.

Manual of correctional standards. New York: The American Correctional Association, 1959.

McCarkle, L. *The Highfields story*. New York: Holt, Rinehart & Winston, 1958.

Montone, E. J. Walton Village: A modified guided group interaction approach. *Quarterly*, 1967, *24*(3), 16–22.

Moreno, J. L. *The first book on group psychotherapy*. New York: Beacon House, 1957.

Nissen, T. *Project span: New careers in community service*. (Project proposal to U.S. Department of Health, Education and Welfare. National Institute of Mental Health). Pomona, Calif.: California State Polytechnic College, Kellogg Unit Foundation, 1970.

Ohmart, H. Institutional preparation for the correctional community. In N. Fenton, E. G. Riemer, & H. A. Wilner (Eds.), *The correctional community: An introduction and guide*. Berkeley, Calif.: University of California Press, 1967, 13–28.

Perls, F. S., Goodman, P., & Hefferline, R. *Gestalt therapy*. New York: Julian Press, 1951.

President's Commission on Law Enforcement and Administration of Justice. *Task Force Report: Corrections.* U. S. Government Printing Office, 1967, 39.

Quay, H. C. Personality dimensions in delinquent males as inferred from the factor analysis of behavior ratings. *Journal of Research in Crime and Delinquency,* 1964, *1.*

Quay, H. C., & Parsons, L. B. *The differential behavioral classification of the juvenile offender. (2nd ed.).* Washington, D. C.: Federal Bureau of Prisons, 1971.

Quay, H. C. & Peterson, D. R. A brief scale for juvenile delinquency, *Journal of Clinical Psychology,* 1958, *14,* 139-142.

Ramirez, J. *TM with drug offenders.* Unpublished research paper, Milan, FCI, 1975.

Roberts, C. F., & Sekel, J. P. *Supplemental follow-up of wards selected in a study of clinical staff appraisal of the eligibility of first admission wards for community retention and rehabilitation.* Sacramento, Calif.: California Youth Authority, Division of Research, 1965.

Rogers, C. *Counseling and psychotherapy.* New York: Houghton-Mifflin, 1942.

Saleebey, G. (Ed.) *The non-prison.* Sacramento, Calif.: Institute for the Study of Crime and Delinquency, 1970.

Saleebey, G. Five years of probation subsidy. *Youth Authority Quarterly,* 1971, 1-19.

Sandhu, H. S. *Modern corrections.* Springfield, Ill.: Charles C Thomas, Publisher, 1974, 204.

Sandhu, H. S. *Modern corrections.* Springfield, Ill.: Charles C Thomas, 1974, 185-198.

Schmideberg, M. Psychotherapy with offenders. In A. R. Roberts (Ed.), *Correctional treatment of the offender.* Springfield, Ill.: Charles C Thomas, 1974, 147-158.

Schmidthofer, E. *Cerebral training: An application of clinical neurophysiology.* New York: Hafner, 1969.

Schultz, W. B. *The FIRO-$_B$ scales manual.* Palo Alto, Calif.: Consulting Psychologists Press, 1967.

Slavson, S. R. *An introduction to group therapy.* New York: The Commonwealth Fund, 1950.

Smith, R. L. *Probation study.* Sacramento, Calif.: Youth and Corrections Agency, 1965.

Sutherland, E. H., & Cressey, D. R. *Criminology.* Philadelphia: J. B. Lippincott, 1970.

Thomas, A. G. The Carkhuff training program. In R. E. Hosford & C. S. Moss (Eds.), *The crumbling walls: Treatment and counseling of prisoners.* Urbana, Ill.: University of Illinois Press, 1975, 35-44.

Truax, C. B., Wargo, D. G., & Silber, L. D. Effects of group psychotherapy with highly accurate empathy and nonpassive warmth upon female institutionalized delinquents. *Journal of Abnormal Psychology,* 1966, *71,* 267–274.

Warren, M. Q. The case for differential treatment of delinquents. *The Annals of the American Academy,* 1969.

Warren, M. Q. *The community treatment project: An integration of theories of causation and correctional practice.* Sacramento, Calif.: California Youth Authority, 1965.

Wilson, G., & Kyland, G. *Social group work practice.* Boston: Houghton-Mifflin, 1949.

Wilson, J. M. and Snodgrass, J. D. The prison code in a therapeutic community. *Journal of Criminal Law, Criminology and Police Science,* 1969, *60*(4), 472–478.

Wichs, R. J. *Correctional psychology.* Canfield Press, 1974, 28.

Wolpe, J. *The practice of behavior therapy.* New York: Pergmon Press, 1969.

Wright, J., & Ralph, G. *A behavioral approach to preventing delinquency.* Springfield, Ill.: Charles C Thomas, 1974.